GLENNA'S ANGEL

A MIRACLE FROM GOD

By

Derrice James

Table of Contents

Dedication

I would first of all like to dedicate this book to God, Jesus, Holy Spirit and the Angel who was sent from Heaven on a Mission for my mum. Without them, there would be no book to write.

Also, to my lovely mum and dad, God bless them.

And of course to my wonderful family,

John, Michael, Mel and Willow

Who have given me so much inspiration and help with putting this book together. I am forever grateful for your prayers, the love, encouragement and support that you have all given me.

I love you all so much.

God bless xxxxx

Acknowledgement

Thank you to the speakers and authors at the "Christian Writers Conference 2022" in Cambridge, who inspired me with their knowledge and encouragement to finish writing this book.

Thank you to Revelation TV, the Christian channel, who played a big part in my mum's Miracle at the time, by interviewing her and showing her Testimony on television. Revelation TV is a blessing to the whole world.

Thank you also to God TV, to Aaron, who happened to call when I was at my computer, with writers block. He asked if I needed prayer for anything and I said, "actually I do." God used him mightily as he prayed the most beautiful prayer, and my writing began to overflow.

Thank you to Judith Corbett, who spent time on the telephone with me, providing me with some of the family background and history relating to the Corbett and Nestor families.

Thank you to Cheryl Ann and the Team at Amazon Pro who worked so hard on publishing this book.

About the Author

Derrice has always had a strong Christian Faith, which has guided her through life. She believes in the Power of Prayer and wants to share her Faith with everyone she meets. God is here for all of us.

She has a heart to help and encourage people to get through the many trials of life, and rejoices when they overcome them.

Introduction

The reason I feel led to write this book is, firstly, I want people to know how wonderful God is, and this book is written to thank Him and let as many people as possible know that in a world where so many things seem out of control, God Himself is here for every one of us, when we call upon His glorious name through Jesus Christ, our Lord and Saviour.

Secondly, I am still in awe of what happened and will never forget it. Every time I think about it, I light up inside and burst with energy! It is still as clear to me all these years later as it was on the day it happened. I have told so many people about my mum's Testimony, and it has really blessed them. It has given hope and faith and lifted up the downhearted. I tell everyone I can because I want people to know that there truly is a God in Heaven who loves us all and cares for every one of us, whoever we are. When I talk about it, I don't like to leave out any details because people don't see the whole picture if you do, but sometimes I feel myself skipping through it because of the time aspect of whoever I may be speaking to, so I thought if I wrote it down, they could read it in their own time. It is not until almost the end of this Testimony that we see the true extent of the Miracle. All the glory belongs to our Lord Jesus Christ.

I believe in Angles. They are a big part of God's Kingdom and are mentioned many times in the Bible. There are realms of Angels in the presence of God Himself, singing and rejoicing in Heaven.

The Bible tells us that they are messengers sent by God to help us on earth. They are here to protect us. At our home, we pray Psalm 91 every day, and I love the verse that says, "Jesus gives His Angels charge over you to protect you wherever you go". [The scriptures used in this book are taken from different Bibles, KJV, NKJV and New English Bible.]

Although I have always believed in Angels and know that they work for God and glorify Him, I have been cautious not to look at them as idols or worship and pray directly to them in any way. Every prayer is through Jesus Christ, and He will send His Angels to assist us in our situations. I always talk to Jesus and pray to Him. I think these days we have to be careful because a lot of people seem to look at Angels like "fairies" or "good luck charms" or "idols", and they can be associated with other things rather than how God created them to be.

I think most of us have had help or an encounter with God's Angels at some time in our lives. Some of us may not even be aware of it, and yet others may not relate the situation to God or His Angels but rather to some unusual happening or supernatural intervention that helped them in their time of need, which they cannot explain. This is a wonderful Testimony of the special encounter my mother had with her very own Angel. I have told so many people about it, and they are really blessed and encouraged, so I wanted to share it to help others. It is far too wonderful to be kept quiet, and I feel so privileged to have been able to witness everything that happened in the ambulance and to know that God sent His Angel on a mission for my mum in her very urgent time of need.

It is often said that many of the people who have had supernatural encounters never talk about it or do not mention it for fear that no one will believe them. Well, I am just the opposite. I love to tell and encourage people about everything that blesses me because I want it to bless them also, and if they don't believe it now, they may refer to it sometime later in their lives. The seed is sown. I cannot contain the miraculous anyway, so I will always talk about it whenever I get the opportunity. There is always someone who needs to hear.

Maybe you feel you have never had any special divine encounter, and it always happens to everyone else. God loves every one of us. Think back over your life; I am sure there is at least one time you can say, "I almost..." My mother had her divine encounter at 79! It's never too late.

This book is about my mother and her beautiful encounter with her Angel. I was so privileged and blessed to be there and witness her Miracle.

In 2007, I started writing a book just on mother's testimony, a little while after it happened, so that we could bless others with it. I sent it off to a publisher at the time, who said they liked it but that it needed to be longer. I left it sitting for many years and didn't do anything with it, but every time I spoke to someone about my mum's testimony, it was as though it was only yesterday that it happened, and I knew I had to do something with it as I felt that it was not my place to keep such a wonderful encounter with God and I knew I had to share it with others to give them hope and encouragement. It didn't belong to us, it was God who blessed us with it, and He wants us to show others that His blessings are for everyone.

My mum and I started writing her own life story some years before. She would dictate while I typed it. I felt bad that we didn't finish it, as time went by and she got older and too tired to do it with me, so her book was left sitting unfinished. I thought I would put the two together, and that is what I have done.

I don't want to ruin things for my readers, so I haven't disclosed some things until later in the book because these things have happened since I started writing it in 2007.

Chapter 1

The Call

I was woken by the sound of my mobile phone ringing beside my bed, totally unaware of the time, as I was still half asleep, but enough to know that it was dark outside. I reached for my phone to see that it was my father calling; it was 6.30 a.m. Friday 6 February 2006. He sounded quite calm, yet anxious and a little confused, as he started to explain that my mum had fainted and did I think he should call an ambulance. "Yes, definitely." I replied. He continued, saying that she had been lying on the floor for a while. I didn't understand why he hadn't called an ambulance in the first place, but at the time, he obviously didn't realise the extent of what had happened to her, and it was typical of my lovely dad, these days, to seek approval or help from his children first before making rash decisions. He said he had already phoned one of my other sisters, and she was on her way as we spoke. I told him I would be over straight away but to call the ambulance as soon as he put the phone down to me, and he assured me that he would. Bless him, he was getting on in years himself, and although he was fit for an 81-year-old, he seemed to be getting more vulnerable and reliant upon his family in his latter years of life, which was noticeable for both him and my mum, and in a funny sort of way quite endearing to see, because now it was our turn to give back, and to look after them, as they had always done for all of us. They had both led very active lives. They were always very organised, and in control, they had to be, having five children to bring up, not to mention the many grandchildren they now have.

My son, who was now also awake, and having overheard some of the conversation from his bedroom, figured out a little of what was going on, and he immediately started to pray. 'Prayer in action'. How blessed we are to be able to call on God anytime, anywhere, with the glorious assurance that He is listening to our prayers 24/7 and watching over us, always here to help us in an instant. Through Jesus Christ, we have His Heavenly Angels sent to minister to us as soon as we pray or even before.

My parents only live about two miles away, so it would take roughly 7 minutes in the car; given it was still early morning and it was quite a straight road, there shouldn't be too much traffic to deal with. I started getting myself ready to go, and although I felt quite shaken by the call, wondering what had actually happened, I was surprised at how calm I was, much calmer than I ever imagined I would be in a situation like this. I didn't really know what to expect or just how serious the situation was, but I knew God could see exactly what was going on, and that was good enough for me.

My son and I prayed together before I left, placing everything in God's hands, as we always do. My son has very strong faith and trust in God; we have been praying together since he was a toddler, and God has answered his prayers in miraculous ways. (I will touch on this later in the book). "Train up a child in the way and he should go, and when he is old, he will not depart from it". (Proverbs 22:6 NKJV).

By now, it was about 6.50 a.m., a typical chilly, misty morning for February. I still felt calm whilst driving to my parents' house, praying, asking God to help us and to make everything all right. I didn't know what I was praying about, but I knew He did, and having the assurance that God is already here in our midst, has even gone before us and is dealing with the situation is overwhelming.

The roads were quite clear, as I had expected. I began to pray in tongues; what a privilege to have this Gift from God, which is available to every believer. I understand now why it is important for us to be equipped with Supernatural Gifts from God. The Bible says the gift of tongues edifies the body and the Church, and when we don't know how to pray or literally cannot find words to pray, it is the Spirit of God interceding for us. "Likewise, the Spirit also helps in our weaknesses. For we do not know what we should pray for as we ought, but the Spirit Himself makes intercession for us with groanings which cannot be uttered." (Romans 8:26 NKJV). The Holy Spirit, who abides in us as believers. God has supplied us with everything we need to get through life on earth; we just have to pick it up and use it. What a wonderful forethought from God when He created us and His World (and gave us His Word). He literally covered all our needs, even the ability to talk to Him directly, to connect to Him in a language He has given us when our minds fall into despair, and we cannot think of any more words to pray. "For he who speaks in a tongue does not speak to men but to God, for no one understands him, however, in the Spirit he speaks mysteries." (1 Corinthians 14:2 NKJV). There is the gift of tongues to be used for private worship and also for the whole body of the church, which should be interpreted for the edification of the church. "But if there is no interpreter, let him keep silent in church, and let him speak to himself and to God". (1 Corinthians 14:28); "And suddenly there came a sound from Heaven, as of a rushing mighty wind, and it filled the whole house where they were sitting. Then there appeared to them divided tongues, as of fire, and one sat upon each of them.

And they were all filled with the Holy Spirit and began to speak with other tongues, as the Spirit gave them utterance." (Acts 2:2-4).

I arrived at the bungalow, its golden lights illuminating in the midst of the night sky. It was hard to believe that in an hour or so, it would be daylight. Every light seemed to be on, and the front door was wide open. I was pleased to see a paramedic's car parked up, half on the kerb, and that help was at hand so quickly. My eldest sister had also arrived. I walked in to find my dad wandering around from room to room, looking lost, trying to find my mum's medication to give to the paramedic, and the expression on my sister's face didn't need words to say that something was seriously wrong. She pointed to my dad's little office, which was once my small bedroom when I lived at home with them.

I walked into the room, not knowing what to expect and with the intention of getting an answer from my mum about her medication, but I wasn't prepared for what I saw. My dear mum was lying flat out on the floor, on her back, but the large mop of strawberry-ginger hair from the kind paramedic who was leaning over her, gently speaking, covered my mum from full view. I was so shocked to see the state of my poor mum. She hadn't just fainted; she looked terribly distressed, extremely anxious and very, very afraid. I can only describe it as like when I once saw an animal on the road, which had been injured when it was hit, and in pain. It had the same desperate look on its face. I still remember it to this day. My mum stared at me with her piercing blue eyes, looking as though she was longing for me to do something to help her. She couldn't get up or speak, and the screeching noises coming from within her were the most frightening noises I have ever heard from any human being. I felt so helpless and totally inadequate, and, for once, I just didn't know what to do. It looked like she was fighting off something that was attacking her. She was trembling, her whole body was trembling, but all the time, her eyes extremely wide open, fixed on me, with tremendous fear as though every part of her inner being was trying to scream out, but something was suppressing her and distorting her speech. She was making excruciating noises, lying on the floor, and she looked in absolute torment. One side of her face looked tight, and the other side had totally dropped, as there were no muscles or substance left. Her hands and fingers were twisted and contorted, and immediately I knew that she had had a massive stroke. I had never seen her like it. I had never seen anything like it. I looked at her and felt so useless, unable to help. Her eyes seemed so full of fear of the unknown, and yet when she connected with me, it seemed like she was trying to tell me something, wanting desperately to communicate but totally unable to. She knew if anyone would have some understanding of what was going on, I would. Surely this cannot be it, I thought to myself; she's shutting down. There is still so much more to know and say, and many things I needed to speak to her about, which I now wish I had done when I had plenty of opportunities to do so. A life can change in an instant. I sat on the floor with her, stroking her trembling legs, telling her not to worry and to calm down and that she would be all right, praying for her from the bottom of my heart at the same time. I was so glad to be next to her, with her at this time of her life, if only to be of some comfort to her knowing we were by her side, and she wasn't alone, and that everything was being done for her that could possibly be done. I know my mum would take comfort in the fact that I was there because she knew 100 per cent that I would be praying.

Chapter 2

Family background

If I can just give you a little background about my mum, to put you in the picture, so to speak. I do not want to keep you in suspense about the main theme of this book, but I feel it is important that you get to know a bit about her, and you will see that God's Grace is for everyone and that Miracles can happen, when we least expect them, to some people who thought they were too unworthy to ever receive.

My Mother was born on 18 April 1926 at the Dufferin Woman's Hospital in Allahabad, India. Allahabad was a medium-sized town in the province of India. (The British Raj). Allahabad was a town very famous to the Hindus because of the two famous rivers of India, which both meet in the town of Allahabad. These are the River Jumna (also spelt Yamuna) and the Ganges. The rivers are very sacred, and every year there is a religious fair held called Mela in which the Hindus come and bathe in order to purify their souls and wash away their sins.

My mother was the eldest of 3 children. She had two younger brothers, Dennis and Billy. Billy being the youngest.

Her father, William Richard Arthur Nestor, was born on 6 June 1894 in a small town called Sultanpore in the United Provence of India. He started his education in the Boys High School at Allahabad and then went on to the La Martiniere School in Lucknow, where he finished his education. After leaving school, he was sent to a very famous engineering school at Jamalpore, where he did a 5-year training course, but after 3 years of being there, he left and joined the United Police Force in India. At the time he enlisted in the Police, they were forming a special unit force of sergeants who were designated in order to deal with the Europeans who lived in India at the time. In those days, when a European committed a crime in India, it was the duty of the superintendent of the Police to deal with the matter and make the arrest. About 30 sergeants were taken on and given special training and authority to make arrests of any European criminals. This allowed the superintendents to carry out more important duties rather than wasting time on trivial matters. These sergeants had to be of European descent, which included English, Scottish, Irish and Welsh. Anyone from the continent at that time who was working in India were all named under the heading 'Europeans', having come from Europe. There was a jail called Nani Jail to which the Europeans were sent to when they were arrested. The police sergeants would arrest and take them there and keep an eye on them.

Her father's side of the family originally came from Ireland, and some settled in India.

One of her ancestors was Jim Corbett, a conservationist; he started his life as a tiger hunter, and I remember my mother telling me stories of how he would go to the villages to hunt the tigers that were taking people out of the villages and eating them. He eventually opened a sanctuary for the animals. We met some of his relations at one of the La Martiniere school reunions in London, which was held every year.

I also recently spoke to one of my mum's cousins, a lovely lady called Judy Corbett, whose father was called Maurice Hugh Nestor, and he lived in Nainital, India. Jim Corbett's brother married her father's aunt, who was a Nestor, and one of her father's uncles married one of Jim Corbett's sisters. So that is how the Nestors and Corbetts became related. The Nestors who went to India originally came from Ireland.

Jim Corbett was at the Treetops, a small hut built on the branches of a giant ficus tree in Keyna, and he was the bodyguard of Princess Elizabeth when she stayed there on 5–6 February 1952 with her husband, The Duke of Edinburgh. Jim had received a call two days before her visit there to say that Princess Elizabeth was graciously pleased to invite him to accompany her to the Tree Tops. He was there to protect her from any of the tigers, lions, or leopards that may be around. It was on the night her father, King George VI died, Elizabeth ascended to the throne and became Queen.

Jim Corbett wrote a book about the Queen's visit, it is called "Tree Tops".

He resided in the Gurney House along with his sister. After he died, the house was transformed into a museum and is known as the Corbett Museum in India.

One of the great legacies of Jim Corbett was the establishment of India's first national park in 1936. Corbett, with a few friends, was instrumental in encouraging the Indian government to create it.

Today the park is known for its tigers and other rare and exotic wildlife and birds and as a popular destination for visitors keen on having a jungle experience. The park is now named after him, Jim Corbett National Park.

♥

Her mother, Coral Grace Nestor, (Richardson being her maiden name) was born on 14 April 1906. She was one of 4 children, who were all born in India, but my mum wasn't sure what part. She was educated first at Bishop Johnson at Allahabad, then went to the Girls High School. She had a very sad life. Coral's mother, Mary (my mum's grandmother) met and married My mum's grandfather (also called William) who at the time worked on the railway. Coral and her siblings were left with their mother, Mary, while their father, William, went to work. Sadly, one day their mother got up to make some milk, and while she was boiling the milk, an open flame caught her long hair alight, and she didn't survive. After their mother's death, their father could not take care of the children as he had to work, so he sent them to boarding school, apart from Coral, who was the youngest, only two years old at the time, she was taken in and looked after by her aunt, who already had 4 daughters of her own.

♥

Coral eventually met and married William Nestor. My mum was the eldest of three children, followed by Dennis, then Billy, who was the youngest. Sadly, her mother, Coral, died from a blood clot in her leg after giving birth to Billy. My mum was only 8 years old at the time.

I remember the conversation I had with my mother when she came over to my house for coffee one afternoon; she poured out her heart to me, telling me all about her life. It wasn't long after I had left home I was the last to fly the nest. It was amazing how my mum actually admitted that she missed me being at home, as when I was there, it seemed that all I did was stress her out and add to her anger. This was the first time we actually sat down together, and she told me things about her life that totally shocked me. I had no idea what a sad life she had, which explained a lot of the reasons why my mum was always so angry and seemingly bitter when we were growing up. I realise now how much pain she had suffered from what she had experienced in her own childhood. My dad would be the one to smooth things over and make excuses for her when she was upset, but looking back, the root of the problems were never dealt with because things weren't spoken about to us in those days; children had no business knowing the personal details of their parents' lives, which was fair enough.

She started to share things with me as if I was one of her best friends. It was so lovely. I was witnessing a new side to my mum, she was so open and chatty, and I saw both compassion and excitement in her that I had never seen before. It was like listening to a story so detailed that I could imagine everything, almost watching a film of her life. She told me that on the day of her own Christening, horse-drawn carriages were waiting to take her and her parents to the Church. This was one of the means of transport in India in those days, called tongas. She said that her mother had said to her father, "Willie, what are we going to name this child?" because up until then, they had still not decided on a name for her. At that time, her father happened to be reading a book on Scotland in which the heroine was called Glenna, so he said to, "give her that name; it's as good as any", and that is how she got her name, Glenna. She was baptised in the Holy Trinity Church at Allahbad by Reverend Cox.

She told me that she also had an elder brother by the name of David, who died when he was six months old of meningitis. He was born on 29 March 1925. I had no idea; I was so sad to hear this; I hadn't heard her speak of him before. She said he was born with a veil over him. Then, even more to my surprise, she said that her mother was also pregnant with another child, and they were travelling on one of the big steam trains in India, when it suddenly braked hard she flew forward off her seat, and as a result, sadly lost the baby. So there should have been five of them. It's amazing that my mum ended up having five children of her own.

I understand now, though, she didn't have her mother's love from 8 years old, she grew up before her time. She said she had to look after her two little brothers. I remember her telling me when we had our chat about how she was playing outside in the garden when they were in India, and she heard nails being hammered into what turned out to be a wooden coffin that her uncles and family were making at the time. She said she went into the front room, and her mother was laying on the settee; and she looked like she was smiling. She didn't even know that she had died. The family standing around her didn't tell her. She had to ask them. How sad. And then she realised that the hammering coffin was for her mother.

Not long after her mother had died, her father married one of the housekeepers they had in India, who already had two children of her own, and they seemed to take first place. It broke my mother's heart, and she didn't forgive her father. I understand now why she seemed so hardened at times; unforgiveness and hurt can do that to you. It can go deep. The woman he married took all my mother's belongings for herself and her daughters, and nothing was left for my mother or her brothers. This made her, understandably, very bitter, and the root of her hatred for her father began and she didn't speak to him anymore. She felt that he favoured his new family and didn't care about her and her brothers. I am sure deep down that he did care.

My mother was a very straightforward person. She spoke her mind and didn't suffer fools lightly. If you upset her, don't cross her path. She would not have forgiven you, and you would be out of her life.

Chapter 3

My mother's younger years

In her teens, my mother went on to La Martiniere School in Lucknow, India. She loved her schooldays, where she had lots of fun and made some lovely lifelong friends. They kept in touch always, either by letter or the odd telephone conversation. They were great letter writers in those days. She was very popular, and she also played Hockey for her school, which led to her playing in the Indian Hockey Team. She was a great inspiration to her friends and the people around her. She had a strong and courageous character, no-nonsense, and a little bit mischievous.

At the age of 18, she joined the Women's Royal Naval Service (WRNS) where she worked in an office in Delhi, India. This was when she met up with my father again (who she had known since she was 11 when they were both living in Lucknow). My father, then 20 years old, was in the British Army stationed in Delhi, and this is where their destiny began. She was very beautiful, and he was very handsome.

They started dating. Looking back at the old black and white photos in the neatly organised albums, which my mum had put together, they looked so smart in their uniforms. All their friends in the photos looked so happy, even though it was wartime you would never have known it, as everyone was literally having a ball, loving the dinner and dances with the big brass live bands, which my mum had a lot to do with organising of course. They were both very good dancers and would jive and jitterbug until the early hours of the morning. The 40s and 50s music was great; everyone seemed to be having a good time, the men pictured with a tumbler of whisky and a cigar in one hand and a beautiful woman in the other.

They would often talk to us about how they met. My dad's version was a little different to my mum's. He was very mischievous and had a brilliant sense of humour. He told us that when he first met my mum, when she was 11 years old, she chased him and kissed him. My mum soon interrupted abruptly with, "No, I didn't; I would never have done that! He kissed me on the cheek, and I slapped him on the face". I think I am inclined to believe my mum. She said my dad and his friends would go to the girl's school and cause havoc. They once shone a big spotlight outside the school at night, and all the girls came out of bed in their nighties. They found this hilarious. And their mischief didn't stop there. In fact, I am amazed that they got away with the things they did. Sometimes I would wonder if they were making it all up, but there was usually someone who was actually there, witnessing it, who could back it up. My dad loved boxing, one of his favourite sports, and he also ran a little boxing club. He had lots of trophies. He said most of them were melted down to make into weapons for the war.

They soon married, and I remember my mum telling me about their Wedding day, how she went on a pushbike to pick flowers from a field nearby her to make up her fresh bouquet on the morning of her wedding. I really felt for her that she didn't have her mother with her on her special day; how different would that have been for her, or a sister to help her, bless her, but she certainly had a lot of very good friends. She was 19 when she and my father got married, and he was 21. She said they had a fabulous wedding, but they had to leave the wedding party, which was in full swing, and go on the train to Lucknow to see my father's parents and siblings as they didn't come to the wedding because it was quite a way, and too far to travel. My mum said they took the top of the wedding cake to his family on the train with them. It must have been hard for my father not to have his mum and dad at his wedding or brothers and sisters, as he was very close to them all.

Not long after they married, my father was posted to Lahore, and that is where their first child, my eldest sister, was born. There was a lot of trouble at the time relating to the partition of India, and people were literally being slaughtered with machetes in front of them. My dad told his dear cook to run away, and gave him some money. It was by chance that another officer friend of theirs managed to get them on of the last military flight out of the new Pakistan, back to India. On his way, he noticed his poor cook laying on the road. Sadly, he didn't make it.

They said they had to leave all their material possessions behind; all my mum took was her sewing machine. She was very creative, and she was an excellent dressmaker/seamstress. The clothes she made were like something out of a magazine or top department store, perfectly and professionally sewn. This led to her later getting lots of work from many women around her, giving orders for her to make their clothes and alterations for their families.

It was quite dangerous then to be there or even get a train or any type of transport. My mother said she wanted to leave India then, but unfortunately, not long after that, my father had a motorbike accident and had to stay there to recover. I can't imagine my mother on the back of a motorbike when I think of them now, but looking back at the old photos, in the 50s in India, it seemed a good way to travel around. Like the old movies on the TV. Although they were tough times, people still seemed to enjoy themselves and live life to the full. My mum often told us how fortunate it was that day they went out on the motorbike because they used to take my eldest sister as a baby, who was their first and only child at the time, on the front of the bike. Can you imagine it? My dad would just strap her to him on the front of the bike. They had decided not to take her with them on that day. My mum said that my dad was "showing off as usual" and tried to go between two lorries that were going the same way. One of his handlebars hit the side of one of the lorry's, and the wheel nuts went into his knee. My mum was thrown off and landed safely, but my dad had bad injuries to his knee and was in the hospital for weeks.

After the partition, they went back to Lucknow to live with my dad's family. My dad spent months recovering from his motorbike accident. He came from a large loving family, and they all lived together in Lawrence Terrace, Lucknow, India. My father was his own mother's favourite, who, although very mischievous, could do no wrong. My mum said that one or two members of his family were not very kind to her and they made her feel like an outsider and it was hard for her, although she got on very well with his parents and one of his sisters in particular, and his brothers.

My dad started to study law and, at the same time, had a little business going making dolls houses and dolls house furniture. He would craft the furniture, and my mum would paint and make the furnishings. I saw the photos, and they were so professionally made. My mum has always been very creative. They also made other wooden toys like hobby horses, so they had a nice little business going.

They then moved to Gouri Bazaar, where my dad worked as a lawyer for the British India Corporation representing the company in cases of employment tribunals. He kept some of his court bundles, and in later years, he would show us delightfully boasting about how impressed the judges would be with the way he presented his cases.

From all their stories we would listen to, it seemed they loved life in India at the time. The Anglo-Indians all lived together, and they had some very close friends; there was a lot of socialising, dancing, parties and good Indian food. My parents had a large house with their own hired cooks and nannies, known then as ayahs, who looked after us all so well. All our meals were cooked for us; that explains why I never followed in my mum's footsteps when it came to cooking; she didn't cook. That is not true; really, she cooked an amazing curry. We also had horses and dogs. When it was very hot, we would sleep outside on the veranda. My dad said he would have to strap us to himself at night in case we were taken by the tigers.

My parents eventually had five children. A son and four daughters. I am a twin to one of them, and we are the youngest. We have listened to many stories of life in India, from the monkeys being chased out of the kitchen to all the games and fun they all had.

Chapter 4
Coming to England

As time went on, most of my parents' Anglo-Indian friends left India and emigrated to England, and my parents eventually followed suit. My mum had great foresight and knew it was the best thing for all of us so we could have a good future. When they eventually left it was hard for my dad to leave his mother and father, and the rest of his family, but my mum wanted her own family to have more opportunities and a good education and pushed forward to moving to England.

Thanks to her persistence, we eventually came to England in 1959. My mother had arranged everything from India. They had a friend in the UK who had sorted out somewhere for us to stay when we first arrived in England; in Finsbury Park, North London, but it was only temporary.

Looking back, my father kept all the booklets from when we came over on the ship. The list of passengers, and there we were, the James family. We were also featured in the ship's magazines. We sailed to England on the Stratheaden, which took six weeks to travel from India to the UK.

We often talked about those days and our journey to England. My mum casually mentioned that my sister had thrown my dummy into the Medeterrain Sea. My sister and I looked at each other at the time in amazement, and I said to her, "How close were we to the edge of the ship? And, what about the barriers?" We laughed. "No Health and Safety Rules then." My brother recalled how he would put his head out of the cabin porthole window at night and look out at the deep dark sea. We were below deck, so it was quite close to the ocean.

There were always plenty of activities going on board the ship for families. My mum even made costumes for us on the boat. Yes, the sewing machine was also with her; like one of her own children, it went everywhere with her. I was dressed in a belly dancer outfit at 18 months old. The children loved dressing up. We were entered into a race with the other toddlers, and apparently, my sister was winning, and I was still at the start line, too timid to do anything. She came back for me, dragged me to the finish line with her, and still won the race. My parents were young and strict but quite cool when I think about it how they managed and coped with everything.

So, getting back to when we arrived in the UK. We stayed for a few weeks at a house that a friend had recommended for us. My dad found a job quite quickly at a firm of accountants while my mum sorted out schools etc. We also had to look for somewhere else to live, and finding somewhere to rent was not easy; people were not so accommodating when it came to putting up a family of 7

My mum eventually went to see a bank manager, who wasn't very cooperative and was unwilling to give us a mortgage. She was told that we hadn't been here long enough to have one. My mum, being my mum, would not take no for an answer, and she told him that she was not leaving until they gave us a mortgage. She later said 'the twins were crying so much, they eventually grated on the manager's nerves, and he ended up giving us a mortgage just to get us out of there." Thanks to mum's determination and persistence. They never once relied on any social benefits help. They eventually bought their own house in Tottenham, North London, a three-bedroom mid-terrace house.

Looking back, my parents worked hard, and they always made sure that we were warm and had food on the table, even if it was only beans on toast or mincemeat, again. We all mucked in and had our chores to do. I remember spending hours holding the long pieces of 4"x4" wood while my dad was sawing away making, yet more, cupboards or shelving or something. It was so boring and tedious, but you dared not show that you were fed up. He was DIY-mad. Then we were all given our paintbrushes, mainly my sister and I, as we were still quite young at the time, as eventually, my older siblings married and left home. I can still smell the putty, which was actually quite a nice smell; it was used to fill in around the window frames; we would love to roll it in our hands and make it into a long piece of string, and my dad would fill it in between the windowpane and glass, holding it in, and then smooth it over and paint the wooden sash windows. My mum was very active too. She would be on the step ladder, pasting and papering the walls and then painting over the wallpaper. We would spend hours on end holding the large double ladders for my dad while he painted the outside of the house, the only house in the street to be painted with several coats of bright red paint, totally covering the beautiful natural brickwork. To add to it, we had a light lavender front door. But that was the fashion in the 60s. Then there was building the garage. Tons of sand and cement and buckets of water to make the base, flattening down the rubble with the pummel and finally, the large, heavy roller smoothing it all over. Now and again, a friend or relative of theirs would pop over to help my dad when we couldn't manage the heavy stuff.

I still remember bathing in an oval-shaped tin bathtub in the garden. And also we had an outside toilet, with newspaper on a string, or rough, slippery toilet paper, which we actually used as tracing paper to draw on. One day a cat had her kittens in there. We watched as she picked them up, one by one, by the scuff of their necks, holding them in her mouth while she carried them over the fence at the bottom of the garden.

My dad built us a paddling pool in the garden. It was only about 5 inches deep and made of concrete and white bathroom tiles. A little bit rough on the feet, but we loved it. We also had an aviary with budgies in it and a couple of goldfish, we believed that we had our very own Zoo.

My sister and I went to school in Tottenham. I will never forget our first day; we were five. My parents took us to the door, and my sister ran off to play in the wendy house, but I cried all day and held the teacher's hand. My mum and dad told us that they felt so bad leaving us they watched us through the window for most of the morning.

At junior school, which was only next door, we had a great drama teacher; she was very enthusiastic. She took our class to the studio, and we made about four adverts for the sweets, Smarties. I remember there were Smarties all over the floor, and children were diving into them, dressed up in fancy dresses and dancing around to the music. We were paid for doing it, about £7, I think. Every time we heard the Smarties advert come on the TV at home, our family would all run into the room and watch it. I think it gave my mum an idea, as soon after this, she got two of my siblings and myself together and spent hours teaching us to sing and dance to a song called Yakatee-yak, with the hope of us becoming the new girl band,

and entering us to a talent competition show, which was on TV in the 60s hosted by Hughie Green, called "Opportunity Knocks". If you won, then you really made it. Unfortunately, my mum's expectations didn't last long; we couldn't sing, and our dancing was, let's say, too uncoordinated, clumsy and totally out of time with each other, and not the most elegant of moves. She eventually gave up and came to the conclusion that it was never going to happen, and her fortune would stay in her sewing machine.

We were brought up with good manners and respect, and love for others. We were too afraid to answer back because they didn't spare the slipper or the feather duster, let alone the odd slap from both my mother and father. They had their rows with each other ok, but when it came to telling one of us off, they seemed to stick together. Rudeness or attitude was not tolerated. I think she thought we favoured my father above her, they were both strict, but he would end up giving us a hug after we had the feather duster flicked on our shins which we used to jump in the air to avoid.

Chapter 5

Greenvale

About five years later, we moved South of the river to a place called Eltham. We lived in a big house on Greenvale Road. High ceilings, four large bedrooms, a front room, a back room and a morning room, not to mention the kitchen and toilet and a huge garden. We weren't materialistic by any means, I don't even think we knew what the word meant, but it was a necessity to have room for all of us as we got older and needed our own space. My eldest sister had now moved out and married, and my parent's first grandson was born.

My dad got a job working as a manager for a food company, and he regularly brought home delicious food for all the family. We were so excited when he came home with a big box filled with minute steaks, melon balls, and lots of other tasty things to cook. We felt like royalty. It made a change from mum's mincemeat, peas and carrots in gravy, or her stews, with meat that didn't dissolve, chewing until it lost its colour and turned into a transparent piece of gristle. We called it 'Everlasting Meat.' We would get up and dance around the room, chewing after she left the room, of course, and then somehow it managed to find its way into a serviette or at the very bottom of the dustbin. She often cooked a curry, which she made a bit milder for us and would put a couple of boiled eggs in it, which was actually quite nice. I remember the time my dad brought home Squid! My mum wouldn't touch them. They lay at the back of the freezer, piled up on top of each other, staring at us every time we opened it. I think they were just for show when friends came round to see how well we were doing.

We loved school dinners; I think we were the only ones who did, as most of the other children at school hated them. Compared to my mums cooking, school dinners were a banquet. She wouldn't mind me saying that. Everything she cooked, she added chillies to and always plenty of salt. Also, the very familiar sound of the butter knife scraping the black char from, yet more, burnt toast. She loved a full flame under her pots and pans. A nice aroma of spices and smoke. Some things you just inherit. And I think I have just that.

Saturday mornings were housework. Again, my parents would give us all our duties to do before getting our sixpence to go and spend at the sweetshop. Yes, sixpence would buy quite a few sweets then. I usually swept the stairs; the others would do dusting and clean the silver or put the window cleaner on the windows, which my dad would later polish off. We had lino in the hallway, so I don't remember us having a hoover, only a carpet sweeper for the carpets in the front room and the back room. And a large broom for the lino. My dad would have every window open and Jim Reeves or Charlie Pride playing loudly through the house. My mum and dad would be singing along as we all did our chores. My mum had a beautiful voice, and the only time she seemed to be really happy was when she was singing in the kitchen, cooking. That was when we were younger. As we all got older and more demanding with our food choices, it all became too much for her to make 5 different dishes, so we were left to get on with it ourselves.

When we first moved to Greenvale, I remember the large marble fireplace in the morning room; it was beautiful. They actually broke up the beautiful marble and made crazy paving out of it for the garden steps and pathway. People couldn't believe that they had done that. Thanks to all the training, we are not too bad at DIY ourselves. Another job we had was breaking up the asbestos roofs in the garden. Yes, asbestos.

My mum started a business from home, making clothes and alterations for people. All of her work contacts were by word of mouth and highly recommended, as there were lots of people in the area who were keen to use her services. She was so good at sewing. We would be watching TV, and my mum would be in the other room sewing until all hours; the machine sounded like a loud engine vibrating through the whole house. Some evenings she would be sitting with us watching TV while she knitted or crocheted. She worked so hard to make whatever small amount of money she could to look after her family. She was so talented and had so much to give.

The socialising from their old days never stopped, and the parties and dances with the big bands continued in the UK, meeting up with their old friends, and we would spend hours listening to the stories they shared when they were younger. She was very active and full of life. They both were. I remember most weekends were spent at parties either at our house or with their friends, most of whom had come over from India now. She also organised lots of dinners and dances, the tickets would always sell out, with live bands, and my sister and I, being the youngest, would always have to go along, and we would count the cigarette ends in the ashtrays and watch the whisky disappear from the glasses of the men who looked very merry, or we would end up sleeping across the chairs until the evening ended. We were never left with babysitters, apart from my eldest sister, who would look after us before she got married and left home.

They must have had some good times back in India during the war with the dances and bands.

They laughed like schoolchildren again, and their friendships were valuable treasures. My mum was an organiser then, and organising stayed with her all her life. She always said she would have been very good in politics and that she would have been a great Priminister or negotiator, and she certainly would have done. She was very strong-minded and so ambitious, but sadly her ambitions stayed in her heart. She had a husband and 5 children to look after. She wanted the best for all of us and tried to realise our individual gifts and bring out the best in us. She certainly was ahead of her time and probably would have had a lot to do with the women's movements today, standing for equal rights and opportunities. She was very liberated in her ways and straight talking and blunt. She would never back down in an argument, and if you knew her, you wouldn't really want to get involved in one.

My mum was so glad to come to England. She kept the habit of shaking her shoes together before she put them on in case a scorpion had got inside. My dad would sit and tell us that he used to fight tigers and elephants in India. We were so intrigued by his stories, which of course, we believed at the time. We sat in awe, listening to them. I think he actually convinced himself that they were true. As young as 7, we believed him, and we would tell our friends at school all about how our dad could fight two tigers with one hand and 10 elephants. I am not sure if they did believe us, but we believed my dad at the time.

My mum was never impressed by anything crude or unladylike. She didn't like my dad telling rude jokes, which would usually be about someone's posterior. She would soon tell him not to be so disgusting. I must have got my mischief from my dad, as I loved a trip to the joke shop and enjoyed placing the soap in the toilet, which turned black on your hands when you used it, a great trick when her friends came over, or the whoopie cushion on the sofa. It didn't go down very well. Also, she was very prudish about things, and my dad would have such a great sense of humour, and she would not find him funny at all. I don't think I ever heard her laugh at any of his jokes, only say how stupid he was, which made us laugh even more. He knew how to press her buttons. As time went on, though, she got more tolerant, especially after her encounter with God, which we will come to soon.

Chapter 6

50 Years in England

My mum always had time for everyone and was full of wisdom and good advice. She helped a lot of her friends who came to the UK later. To settle in. She kept in touch with a lot of her friends from India, especially her school friends who had also come to England. Every year they attended the La Martiniere School Reunion's here in London, and she was on the committee helping with arranging the events. It was so lovely to go along and meet all her friends. We had a lovely lunch in one of the hotels in London, an Indian Banquet. Apart from the food, it was just like any school reunion only most of them were now in their 70s and 80s, it was lovely to see. They started meeting up when they first came over from India. Only as the years went on, there were fewer and fewer of her friends attending; either they were too frail or had gone on to glory. How cheeky they must have been at school, and some of her friends still had that mischief. Also, my mum did when she got together with them. My dad stopped going to them, and she was happy about that because she could be herself and not have to worry about him or have to listen to how much better his school was, as they would argue.

♥

She loved gardening; you could see her creativity in her garden, the colours and flowers and her little touches everywhere. She even painted the gnomes, and she loved Roses; they were her favourite flowers. The garden was full of colour and life. She certainly had green fingers. My dad made birdhouses and window boxes, which were really lovely, and he gave them to all of his children for their gardens.

My mum was very creative and would keep most of the greeting cards that she was given over the years and would use them to make Christmas gift tags or bookmarks. She kept everything. In fact, she was a bit of a hoarder, bits of paper, even the cellophane wrappers from cards which she would use to put her stamp collection in. She re-used everything she could. She also gave lots to the local primary school for the children to use in art. She loved sewing by hand as well, it looked like she had used the sewing machine, it was so neat and tidy, and she had so much patience with her hobbies. She was a fabulous dressmaker and made all of our clothes. She taught herself, or rather she had a natural gift from God.

The house was always open to friends and always a curry on the go, which they could cook up from nothing, it seemed, but the ingredients were always in the cupboard. My mum would have great patience when it came to slicing the onions into tiny pieces and browning them with the spices in the pan, the smell was delicious.

They went through a lot in those days, and yet that generation found nothing was too much for them. They just got on with it and were always there for one another.

Recently my dad said if only they had FaceTime when his parents were alive. He could have kept in touch with them rather than just the letters. It was hard for my father to leave India, as he was leaving behind his dear parents and siblings and many friends. My mother, on the other hand, had great insight, as she wanted a better life for us all, and as many of their Anglo-Indian friends had done, she knew she had to move abroad; it was either Australia, Canada or England. The land of opportunities. Life would have been very different if they had not made that decision all those years ago. Her brothers grew up and eventually married, one moved to New Zealand, and the other went to England. She couldn't stand the heat anymore, and all was too much for her. She said when she was pregnant with my twin sister and me; she went up to the Himalayan mountains where it was cooler. She knew about the new life she wanted for us all, as some of her friends had gone before her and written her letters upon letters saying to come to England.

In April 2009, it was the 50th anniversary of our coming to England. We boarded the ship, the Stratheaden, in April 1959 and never looked back. My parents, my siblings and I went to celebrate at an authentic Indian restaurant in Plumstead. The day we went to celebrate I thought, as it was a special occasion, I should have brought a present for them. I was running late as usual and knew I didn't have time to stop and buy something on the way. I then felt very strongly that God was speaking to my heart, "Write a Poem". I was not any good at writing poems, but the feeling in my heart was so strong. I knew it was from God. I quickly grabbed a pen and a piece of paper, and a poem immediately came to my mind, and it flowed like a river. I typed it up, gave it a pretty fancy edging that made it look like it was typed on a scroll, printed it off and then laminated it. This poem actually explained everything. If I had seen it in a shop, I would have bought it because it described their lives. I couldn't have written it on my own without the help of the Holy Spirit. This is the poem:

<u>**50 YEARS TODAY**</u>

It must have been a hard decision to make that day,

Whether to go, or whether to stay,

But the troubles were rising all around,

And you needed your family to be safe and sound.

You left behind your childhood days,

Good times and sad times, in different ways,

But your family and friends knew only too well

That it was with God's blessing, we all would sail.

On board the Stratheden, we sailed on the sea,

Wondering how our new lives would be,

But with a Mother and Father so full of love, and care,

We knew we would make it, anywhere.

It must have been so difficult for you both,

But you went ahead, and made the most,

To come to a strange country, with 5 little faces,

Nowhere to live, and just our suitcases.

But to you both we owe, everything we are,

We have been given the chance to become a star,

I know times have been difficult, and we have had our troubles,

But they've always ended in kisses and cuddles,

So to God, to you Mum and Dad, we say THANK YOU,

For giving your lives for us all, and giving us the opportunities

We may have never had, had you not made that decision

all those years ago.

My mum and dad loved it and put it on their wall. So it made me realise that you don't always have to spend a lot of money, gifts from the heart are free. Especially blessed when given by God.

We had a lovely meal and celebrated our 50 years of being in England.

Chapter 7

Mother's Intuition

My mum tried to convince me to do a typing course when I was a teenager. "It's something you can always fall back on, and you will always have work." She would say. I told her that I would NEVER work in an office. I was a free spirit. I couldn't be tied down in an office; not for me. She eventually persuaded me, and I started the typing course, also because my sister was doing it at evening school, and to please my mum, of course, but I didn't end up finishing the course as I found it too boring. I just learned the keyboard 'asdf' with the left hand and ';lkj' with the right. I remember it well. Touch-typing. "I will never use the numbers," I thought, so I didn't bother to learn them, as I had no intention of being a typist. I have been working in an office for the past 45 years as a PA Secretary, by the way, and have worked in some of the top law firms in London, using my touch-typing skills. So thank you, mum. And if only I had leaned the numbers at the time, it would have made things a lot easier now.

♥

As I said, she was an excellent seamstress and made all of our clothes and her own. She always looked so immaculate and glamorous without even trying. She was slim and had a good pair of legs on her, as she would always say. The only make-up she wore was face powder and bright red lipstick, which complimented her dark brown hair and beautifully smooth pale complexion, and bright blue eyes. She was comfortable around the house in a pair of summer slacks and a nice blouse. When she and my father went to the dances, they looked like something out of Hollywood.

When we were young, she stayed at home and looked after us all, earned some extra money from doing alterations and would have people knocking on the door at different times bringing their suites and dresses for alterations.

She kept her Anglo-Indian accent all of her life. Friends used to say, "Your mum has an accent". They were quite surprised when I said it was Indian. I think they thought she was Australian. It was still very strong, especially when she got angry with my dad.

My dad was very active, too; together, they made a great pair, but my dad always seemed more sensitive, and my mum always seemed to be harder in character, but underneath she was quite soft.

♥

I remember when I was very young I started going to Sunday School, and it was there that I really learned about Jesus. He was always kind and loving, and I used to colour in the picture books, thinking what a lovely friend He is. He became my best friend, and I have trusted Him ever since. How He loves everyone and has so much compassion for people. He is now my friend, forever.

My mother wasn't an atheist; I knew she believed in God. We used to go to Church as a family when we were young, especially on Easter and Christmas Eve. It was lovely when it was snowing, and we would go to Midnight Mass in our best clothes. When we came back from Church, my dad would put the turkey in the oven to cook slowly on low heat all night.

At Christmas, when we were young, my dad would dress up as Father Christmas and come in with presents for us at our home, and we had no idea that he was actually our dad. We would be very shy of Santa, and when Santa left and my dad eventually came into the room, dressed as himself, we would tell him that we just saw Santa. We never quite put it together that he was never in the room at the same time as Santa.

At Easter, on Good Friday, we would fast for three hours from 12-3 O'clock and then eat Hot Cross Buns, afterwards. I remember once, when I was quite young, feeling so hungry, so I ate a chocolate biscuit while fasting and felt so bad about it. I still remember it. Easter Sunday we would go to Church to celebrate, "Jesus has Risen".

♥

We didn't have a washing machine with a family of 7. Black bags full of laundry were loaded onto a pushchair, and we would spend hours on end in the launderette waiting for the washing to dry, adding what seemed like a never-ending stream of coins into the machines. We would often meet our friends there, stay warm by the dryers and chat while waiting for the washing and drying to finish.

Another unusual thing my mum did was lay out all the clean white laundry, that she had hand washed at home, on the grass in the back garden to dry. Our neighbour never did understand why. My mum said they used to do it in India; it made the whites whiter. I never knew what to believe, sometimes you think it was a story, but in fact, it was the truth, some of the most bizarre things.

She wouldn't even leave her underwear on the washing line; she would take it in if anyone came over. It was not appropriate for anyone to see it.

♥

Our school shoes were bought at Clarks shoe shop. I still remember clearly the advert on the TV, in black and white, and the girls climbing over the rocks, "Tough Go-Girl Shoes". The boys shoes had a compass in them if I remember correctly. Our parents bought us the same shoes every time the old ones wore out. They were the only shoes that lasted and were good value for money. But before we got our new ones, we had to wait until they were really worn out, and "Tough-Go-Girl shoes" didn't wear out very quickly. When they did, we could literally feel the pavement through the bottom of them. Sometimes my parents would buy rubber soles and stick them on with rubber glue, until we went back to the shoe shop. Our inner soles were cut out, using cardboard. How happy we were to get a new piece of cardboard in our shoes. And what a wonderful feeling to get a new pair of shoes.

There were some girls at the school that went to the trendy shoe shops and would show off their fashionable shoes, but it was always Clarks for us.

♥

Chapter 8

Difficult times

Going back to when we lived in Greenvale, my mother went through a difficult time, what we now realise to have been 'the Change' or 'Menopause', and she suffered a lot from depression. My mum would be in bed most of the time, in a dark room, curtains drawn, and she also suffered from migraine headaches. Back in the 60s, we didn't understand what was going on, and my mother was put on a drug called 'Valium' which we didn't realise at the time was actually doing to her. She was in her 40's then.

She went through a terrible time living in the torment of her past and being eaten up with unforgiveness. She would say things, and we were too young to understand or even believe if they were true. My father seemed to be the patient one, but thinking back, he probably wound her up, and he was able to be calmer, but my mother would go into rages. Sometimes we didn't know what we would come home to after school. My father's clothes were all over the floor, and row after row. We even came back to see baked beans all up the wall where she had thrown them out of the saucepan. She was always accusing him of infidelity at the beginning of their marriage in India, but he would dismiss it as though it was all in her mind. Because she was so angry all the time and he seemed the calm one, I'm sorry to say, but we would listen to him, but not want to take sides anyway. My mother became so full of hatred, and yet I would see my father praying every morning before he went to work, something that I will never forget. My father always denied it and said it was a friend that came to the house, and my mother didn't like her.

My mum even left home once, I was about 10 at the time, and I recently found the hand-written letters she kept that I had written to her asking her to come home, saying we missed her and asking her if she was cold. And also, 'who was going to buy our shoes for us?' Those Clarks shoes left a scar, I think. (Only joking) She kept my letters for all those years. This is a typed version of one of the letters, with the spelling mistakes, bad grammar and all, it reads:

To Darling Mummy, All of us have missed you a very lot. Please will you come back and stay with us for ever because I and we miss you very much. I have been playing nearly evry day with next door. I don't do much when it is time for bed for next door I only sit and watch telly. I hope you are not lonely at night or cold. I miss you very much. And mummy who is bying our shoes. I am very sad without you and so is all of us. Nearly every day I cry for you to come back. Daddy wants to make up with you will you make-up next time. I hope you have injoyed this letter but this is not the end of this letter. One day before or come on our party. If you come back I will be very happy and so will all of us. Please will you write to me and I hope you have injoyed this letter now I must say good night and I will see you soon. With all our love Derrice, Daddy, xxxxx

My sister and I went to stay the night with her at the flat she was renting; it was cold and dank and had a shared bathroom. It was just a room, really. She seemed so lonely there, but we were too young to speak to her about it all.

I remember she came back to Greenvale for our birthday, and when she was leaving, my dad pleaded with her to come back home. I remember her crying at the door, pulling away, and how sad we were to see her go. Thankfully, not long after that, she came back home.

Growing up, though, she always seemed so angry, and my parents seemed to argue a lot fiercely, and there were times I would have to pull them apart. We were either coming in to or waking up to shouting arguments. There were so many fun family times and yet just as many arguments, it seemed.

Looking back now, I realise that because she was so eaten up with bitterness and anger, I don't really think she could appreciate just what she had around her. We loved her very much, but she always seemed to be on edge. She was weighed down by it, but when she was released after her encounter with God, you could see the difference and freedom she embraced in life in its fullness, appreciating everything around her.

I remember one evening, my sister and myself were playing at our next-door neighbours' house when we suddenly heard a loud sound. We all came rushing out to the front garden, and my mum had smashed her front bedroom window with a hammer. She was arguing with my dad. We were too young to actually do anything about it, but I remember going back home to find my mother in a rage of anger and tears. I always felt helpless to do anything as my dad seemed to be the one who was trying to calm her down when we got there. And she was physically very strong. You could feel the tension in her if you touched her.

I'm telling you these things because I want to give you a picture of what she was like before Jesus touched her.

Another time, I was woken to the sound of them arguing in the hallway, by the bathroom. It was quite late in the evening. I remember getting out of bed to find her in her nightdress with a hand full of tablets in one hand, and a medicine bottle in the other, throwing her head back, mouth wide open, into which she began pouring the tablets, and then she shut and locked the bathroom door. My dad tried to hold the door open, but as I said, she was very strong and managed to shut it. She had taken an overdose. I remember we were trying to get her out, and then my dad called for an ambulance. The next thing I remember was the ambulance taking her away, and my father went with her.

I walked into the hospital later that night, early morning, to see my dad sitting alone in the corridor. He said they had given her a stomach pump. I don't think she would have done that again. She told me afterwards that it was a terrible experience. How sad and broken she must have felt to do the things she was doing. The Valium had a lot to do with it as well, we found out later, mixed with a lot of hurt and unforgiveness.

We couldn't seem to do anything that helped when they argued; When we eventually went into the room where they were arguing, my dad would seem like he was trying to calm her down. Sometimes he would ask my older sister to call my mums sister in law, who didn't live too far away, but I think that was to try to help my dad more so that he could cope; I do think sometimes he had a lot to do with her getting into a rage in the first place, although admittedly, it didn't seem like it took much for her to get into one. My dad would tell us that she had Munchausen's and wanted attention. We didn't really know what that meant, but he made it seem that it was all in her mind. Although it really wasn't.

One time I walked into one of their arguments to find my mum hammering her wedding and eternity rings, smashing them individually with the hammer, squashing them so much that the gold wedding band touched in the middle, and most of the diamonds in the eternity ring had popped out. It upsets me to write this, with almost an element of disloyalty to my mum, but unless I mention these things, you won't get to see what a change there was in my mum after her encounter with God, and besides, I know that she wouldn't mind me saying it. As it happened, some years later, I went to an evening jewellery class, and I managed to have the rings fixed, which I later gave to my father, and he gave back to my mum on their wedding anniversary. So there was a happy ending as she did actually wear them again. I think she must have secretly missed them. She never bought my dad an anniversary card for as far back as I can remember or a birthday card, but he always bought her beautiful cards with lovely words and a bunch of red roses. Looking back, she must have had a good reason not to get him a card. She certainly wasn't a hypocrite.

The rows were unbearable at times; we don't know how they had the energy to row so much. They were both quite highly strung, but you never actually knew what started the rows, but suddenly you would hear my mum shouting, like, I hate to say it, but like she was possessed. We really didn't want to leave the house at times, and the rows would go on for ages. I was worried about what my mum might do.

Chapter 9

Dads Retirement

As time went on, my mum and dad moved from our big house in Greenvale into a Bungalow. My mum found the house too much to clean and wanted to downsize, again, thinking about the future. My sister and I moved with them, but eventually, we moved out and started our own lives and left them to it. They seemed to be getting on a bit better and acting like elderly people should do, watching TV and having meals together. It was so nice to see. There was the odd time, though, I must admit, I put the key in their front door to hear an argument going on, and I turned around and walked back out again, quietly closing the door behind me, and they didn't know I had been. It wasn't a really bad row like they had when they were younger, but a mellowed row, which was still quite unbearable to listen to.

Most of the time, I would try to make them make up, as when they had an argument, they wouldn't talk for months on end, and it seemed such a waste of time. The only bonus of them not talking (more so when we lived at home) was that we got away with a bit more, as they were nicer to us, bouncing off one another and using us in the middle. "Ask your mother if she wants some tea". However, my mother wouldn't ever say that the other way around. I used to push them together or try to make them hold hands, and she never liked me doing that. My father would always laugh as he would try and make up by making her some tea. He had such an amazing sense of humour. I think the neighbours were used to hearing their rows, but they would never say anything and were always polite when we saw them. Yet they must have heard hours of heated arguments and the odd swear words.

Not long after my dad retired, he had to have a triple heart bypass. My mum had been staying with one of her friends for a couple of days while my dad was in the hospital. I took her to see him when he was in intensive care, and my mum started to talk to him about her time with her friend; she was very excited. He gestured to her with his hand to speak a bit quieter, and suddenly she flared up, shouting at him in anger, and everyone in intensive care, including the staff, looked around in shock. She then stormed out of intensive care, and I looked at my dad, who had wires coming out from all over the place and felt so sorry for him. I went to find my mum, who was nowhere to be seen. I didn't want to leave my dad worrying about her, so I went back in and told him that I had found her and that she was sitting outside on a seat. I wanted to make sure he was calm when I left him as he had just had major heart surgery. I drove around the streets, crying at what had just happened and looking for my mum, but I didn't find her. It turned out that she had got on a bus and gone home. I was 8 months pregnant at the time and really didn't need to be doing that.

♥

As time passed by, my mum was getting a little bit more used to my dad being retired, and they seemed a lot more chilled out, although my mum wouldn't agree, having him around her feet all day, as she would say, we would all meet at our parents' house on Saturdays for a family gathering and my parents would cook a lovely curry and more and more grandchildren arrived and the family expanded by the year. We had nice times, playing music on the stereo and sitting around in the garden chatting, even dancing to some of the old rock and roll music. As more and more of us came over, we ended up bringing food to help out, so it wasn't too much for my parents. We took turns washing up and making the tea. My parents mellowed a lot more even but still had their arguments; they were both very fiery. They seemed a bit more content, but my mum was still very proud and stern at times, but they looked forward to the family visits at the weekend, although I think as they got older, they were pleased for the peace and quiet when we all left.

Chapter 10
Pentecostal Church Meeting

I gave up work when I had my son. When he started nursery I wanted him to go to a Church of England school, as I felt it is a good foundation to have, and the nursery I found also had a junior school attached to it, which he also went to, and was near to where we lived at the time, and it was connected to the local Church, which was a High Church of England. The Vicar would come in and take assembly every morning, which parents were also allowed to attend, as the Church was connected to the school, and so I got more involved and loved every minute of it. My son is very close to God and has a lot of faith.

There was a local Church meeting being held in a park nearby which had lots going on for children and adults. There was also a pastor who attended the meetings who was a healing evangelist. One of the school mums told me about it and said people were getting healed there. I was used to the Church of England and had never been to a Pentecostal Church before. The meeting was held in a large tent. Out of interest, I went to see what it was all about. When I went into the tent where the pastor was preaching, there were lots of people jumping and dancing around and singing, and some people were laying on the floor, some falling to the floor as I watched. I was not sure what it was all about, but I was intrigued. I sat and listened to the sermon, which I thought was very good. As I was sitting there, people were still making a lot of noise, some shouting, some crying and laughing, I couldn't get my head around what was happening and wondered if this really was of God.

A little later in the evening, people started to move the chairs out of the way to make a large space in the middle of the tent, and the pastor, who was still preaching with the microphone in his hand, started walking over to people praying at the same time, and when he got near to some of them, they were falling to the floor. I watched a woman on the floor near where I sat; she was rolling around, laughing. I was very concerned as I didn't know what was happening with her, but I knew I didn't want any of it, especially not having the pastor come and pray for me, so I went to the very back of the tent. My father and some of my church friends were with me.

He walked through the meeting and was heading for the back of the tent, still praying for people on his way with one hand in the air and the microphone in the other and some people were falling to the floor, shaking, letting out noises of laughter or shouting. I could see that my dad was looking somewhat concerned. Then the pastor came over to me, he looked straight at me, pointing with his finger and spoke to me directly about things that had been going on in my life at the time, which he was totally precise about. He said that I had been very hurt but that God loved me and had seen all the things I had been going through, and that I should stay on His path. Then he put his hand up, never touched me at all, and I fell to the floor. The power. I was very with it and not knocked out as I thought I may have been, and I soon picked myself up. I realised that I hadn't hurt myself when I fell and that I was very aware of what was going on. This was new to me, and it was real, but I was not sure about it. I didn't understand it, but thanks to this very meeting, I suddenly had a desire and hunger to know more, and it started me on an amazing spiritual journey, and I never looked back. I began to understand and to know God in the most powerful way. I was able to speak to people about things I had questioned all my life, and they had the answers. People who had experienced similar things and understood and explained things I had been searching for. And my spiritual journey with Jesus became enhanced.

♥

I found a Pentecostal Church, which I loved. I was not used to praying standing with my arms up in the air, so it took a while to get used to it instead of praying with my head in my hands. I was amazed at how people were outwardly praising and worshipping God, showing their deepest love for Him. In the Church of England, it was very private, and also very nice and more personal, but these people really loved God and were actually encountering His presence and His love. Some of them stood up boldly, thanking God and praising His name. There were people speaking in tongues and prophesying. The pastor's sermons were full of wisdom and knowledge, and I actually began to learn and understand the Bible a lot more clearly through these teachings. Something that I had not really experienced before as the Church of England had the same sheet every week with different sermons, and I did love it; I loved the presence of God in the Church of England and the intimacy with God, where I would take all my prayers to Him in private. But these people were praying out loud, and that was ok too.

♥

It brings me to a time, when a friend I once worked with came into the office one day and started to tell me about a Church she had been to in London, she was in awe of everything she experienced there. She said she attended the Alpha Course and started to explain about it all. I wasn't sure that what she was saying was right, and to top it all off, one of the London magazines did a feature on it at the time, which I showed, to my friend, in an unapproving manner. She tried to tell me that it was the best thing she had experienced and I feel ashamed to say that I doubted everything she told me about it. How narrow minded of me, and how dare I judge the move of God. It taught me a lot and never to criticise what I didn't understand. Now, all these years later, I know exactly how excited she was, and how it changed her life, and how it changed and enhanced mine.

♥

Since my father had retired, he loved coming to the prayer meetings and seeing the evangelists and my dad and some lovely friends that I made at church, joined me, and we started a journey together, which was very exciting. I did ask my mum to come, but she wouldn't come. She had heard about the Pentecostal church when we lived in India and knew people who went there and thought it was a cult. I tried to assure her that it wasn't, but she was very adamant and didn't want to know. She was not very happy that we were going either. When I think back now, it may have had something to do with the fact that my father's sister was a missionary in India in a Pentecostal church, and I don't think that they got on very well. My mother found a lot of hypocrisy in the Church, which I could not disagree with.

Although my dad stayed at his local Church of England, he would come to some of the church meetings or conferences, and I began going to see different pastors who were preaching from different countries when they came from all over the world to preach in the UK and going to the meetings. I loved the worship music and soaking in the beautiful presence of our dear Lord Jesus. It was nice when other Christians would come and give a word of knowledge about how God is going to use you or how much Jesus loves you. I loved everything. I wondered why I hadn't found the Pentecostal church all those years ago. Nothing against the Church of England, of course, but the Pentecostal church was just what I needed, just what I was always looking for, and I felt totally complete and at home there. It was alive and full of the Power of The Holy Spirit. Everything made sense to me. We never understood the Power of the Holy Spirit before.

I started reading a lot of books, which is something I had never done and going to small Bible group in London, learning all about the Bible, and my father and friends came with me to some of the meetings as well. We even went on the Alpha Course, which was lovely. My mother stayed at home, and we didn't really appreciate how she must have felt. Looking back now, it must have been very hard for her to see us all going off in the car. We asked her lots of times, but she wouldn't come and had nothing to do with it.

♥

My father got baptised at age 75. My mother didn't come, but some of the family did. In a way, she pushed herself away, but we didn't see it, as really she needed God and seemed to be denying herself, maybe because of a little pride or whatever had upset her in her past.

Now and again, when we were on our own, my mum would sometimes chat with me about her own spiritual experiences. She said, "I know people don't think I believe in God, but he has helped me most of my life. There was a time when I was so down, and God was there." She pointed to a silk flower display that was in her room, and she said she had a vision of Jesus in the flowers. She also said she had a dream one night that she was walking with Jesus; she described what He was wearing and the colour of His sash around his waist. She said they were walking through the forest together, talking. I think she knew she could talk to me because I believed her, and it seemed like she thought other people didn't think she could have had such experiences with God because she didn't go to Church or openly discuss things. It must have been very difficult for her to think back now. No one meant to make her feel left out, but she didn't want to come along with us; she made it very clear and could be quite stubborn about things she didn't want to do, and no one could make her do it.

She used to say that she would argue with God and ask him why with certain things happened. She had no fear of anyone. But God understood her.

Chapter 11

Forgiveness

I was flicking through the channels on the TV one day, and by chance, I found a Christian channel. I was so excited and amazed. It was called the God Channel. What a blessing. There were lots of teachings on it and sermons from various ministries. Films on the Bible about Jesus, and the books of Daniel, Moses, and the whole Bible.

I watched a testimony of a man called Ian McCormack. He was being interviewed by a lovely man called Howard Conder. 'My Glimpse of Eternity' was about Ian McCormack, who had a near-death experience after being stung five times by a Box Jellyfish, and he went to Hell and Heaven and met Jesus. It changed his life, and he now goes around the world telling people about it to help them and bring them to salvation. It was such a powerful testimony. I was absorbed with it. What a blessing. I ordered several copies of the video and gave them out to people to bless them with it. This lovely man was telling the truth. He had unforgiveness, and he said that Jesus showed him that he had to forgive. It made me think about my mum, and I was worried about her as she had so much built up inside her and was oozing unforgiveness.

I took a copy of the video to my mum and dad's house and put it on, and I said to my mum that she had to watch it. We sat down with my father, and we all watched it together. I sat behind my mum's chair and watched the tears falling down her cheeks when it came to the part about forgiveness. How you must let go and forgive those who have hurt you. I had never ever seen her so touched; she was even shaking slightly, and that hard shell was breaking down.

After the testimony finished, she cried from the bottom of her heart, and I saw the breakthrough in her life. I said to her how important it is to forgive; whoever hurt her, she must forgive them. She said she had forgiven them now, I think she must have done it while listening to the video when Ian was leading the prayer of forgiveness at the end, and the instant release in her was unbelievable to see. She forgave, and there was a change in her that everyone could see. She was free and so much happier. She laughed and actually had joy in her heart.

♥

It was so lovely to visit my parents, and my mum would now get involved in the Bible discussions. She would give her point of view and experiences and was enjoying being part of it all. Unfortunately, though, as time went on, some of the discussions with my dad ended up in arguments. She again began to feel like an outsider, and the discussions seemed to turn into more of a competition about who knew more about the Bible and whose opinion was correct. I never like to argue about the Bible, discuss yes, but not a challenge on who knows more or who is well-read. The Bible actually says, "Accept other believers who are weak in faith and don't argue with them about what they think is right or wrong." (Romans 14:1 NLT).

Eventually, she stopped getting involved again, which was a shame. I didn't want to get involved either, but we would have our own discussions when we got together. We would chat on our own about things, and she said God helped her to get us all to the UK.

She had a glowing figure of Mary in her room that looked like Jesus with his arms out, and she took great comfort in it.

♥

As time went on and my parents were in their late 70s, she was less angry about everything and much more content and happy in general, but still a little feisty underneath.

It helped to have my son and his younger cousin around as she got on very well with them, and they would have sleepovers at my parent's house and have lots of fun; they being the younger generation, brought out the best in them and moved them on with the times.

My mother and father were finally happy elderly grandparents enjoying life as they deserved. They were great with all their grandchildren, and they were far more tolerant grandparents than they were parents.

They became more chilled out about everything and slowed down a lot, as you should do, enjoying the family, and my mum would love to come out on her own with us for shopping or for a meal. She didn't want my dad to come, so we would take him shopping separately. He didn't go for a meal to a restaurant; he liked going to McDonald's.

Chapter 12

Angel Encounter

in the Ambulance

The ambulance arrived very quickly, and before we knew it, two more paramedics were there; one was the driver, and the other one was carrying a stretcher to take my mum to the hospital. I left the room so they could attend to her.

In the meantime, my sister and my dad had found the medication, but we didn't have a clue what was what; there was so much of it in the box. My mum was very organised and particular with everything she did, but what we needed now was a clear list of her medication, explaining in detail exactly what it was and when it was needed, so we could relay it to the paramedics to give them some idea of her medical history, as a matter of urgency. To us, it was just a jumble of boxes with labels and names we couldn't even begin to start to pronounce. Too late for that now; if only we could ask her, she would know straight away and be telling the paramedics everything. Who would have thought we needed it in a situation like this anyway.

While the paramedics were attending to my mum, I was asking my father what had happened. He said she got up to go to the toilet at around 6.00 a.m. Ten minutes had passed, and she had not come back to bed, so he went to the bathroom door to check on her. The door was almost closed, so he didn't want to disturb her, and she wouldn't have liked being disturbed anyway, so he went back to bed. He said another ten minutes or so had passed, and she still had not come back to bed, so he went again to the bathroom door and called out to see if she was all right. He could hear noises, so he thought she was OK. Again, he went back to bed. He said he was concerned when she still didn't come back to bed after another ten minutes had passed, so he felt he had to get up and check on her. He went back to the bathroom, and this time he opened the door, but she was not in there. Then he realised that the noises seemed to be coming from his little office, which was next to the bathroom, so he went to have a look. When he opened the door, there she was, lying on the floor. She had been on the floor for almost half an hour before my dad had realised. He must have been so afraid himself when he saw her. He said he immediately prayed for her, then brought her a pillow and supported her head. He put his Bible on her pillow, then phoned my sister and me.

My dad has always been a great inspiration for us as a family. As I said, from a very small child we watched him kneeling down in prayer in his suit every morning before going to work. We have been brought up in a Christian home. We went to Church and Sunday school. I am not claiming that we are the perfect family by any means, and we have had many challenges along the way, as most families do, but when the foundation is laid on God's Word, The Holy Bible, and Trust and Faith in our Lord Jesus Christ when it comes to the crunch, you will see an answer to prayer. Jesus Christ has always been part of our lives and in our household.

One of The paramedics who arrived in the ambulance came and asked us about my mum's medication again, but as we said to the other paramedic, we didn't really know without looking through the box, so we handed the box of medication to him. It really makes you realise how important it is to have these things properly sorted out.

The paramedics said that my mum needed to get to the hospital immediately as it was very serious. I asked if it was a stroke, and they thought so, but obviously could not say, but she needed to get to the hospital urgently. They decided to go to the nearest hospital, which wasn't the one we usually went to, but it was closer. I asked if she could go to the one we usually use, as I knew she would prefer it, but they said she was very sick and needed to get there as soon as possible, and of course, we agreed. They took my mum out on the stretcher, still screeching and looking totally unaware of what was going on with her, and they then settled her into the ambulance.

I turned to my dad and sister at the front door and said, "Let's pray", and we held hands, and my dad prayed for my mum. We knew God would help us, and only He knew what the situation was. By praying, we invite and ask God to intervene. After all, He is the Great Physician who designed us in the first place.

The paramedics were so lovely. They all arrived so quickly and were very caring. We felt very comfortable with them, almost like we knew them. The lady paramedic asked me if I wanted her to take my dad to the hospital in her car, but I said my sister was going to take him, and I thanked her for all she had done, and we hugged and said goodbye at the back doors of the ambulance.

I went in the ambulance with my mum. Once the paramedic had finally settled her in, he came over to me and fastened my seatbelt. The blue lights lit up, and off we went. I looked over at my poor mum, who seemed so helpless and vulnerable lying there, and I just wanted to turn everything back to where it should be. What was she experiencing? Was she as frightened as she looked? What was she trying to tell us? What was going on in her mind? Was she even aware of what was going on? It seemed that, although she was so close, I could sense a giant vacuum consuming her, pulling her upwards, and that she was going high up away from me, and I was helpless to do anything. All sorts of things go through your mind; will we ever be able to communicate again? Is this it? The things that you should have said and done. What is going to happen now? Where will she go?

She was still very distressed in the ambulance, twisting and making noises, unable to speak, and her eyes very wide open, looking all over the place and then just staring. I just wanted my mum to be my mum again; I want her back; this is not how it was supposed to be; this wasn't my mum; it wasn't her to look like this; I so wanted to help her and knew that she was thinking she could count on me, but now this was out of my control.

The paramedic in the back with us was so warm and kind. He spoke to my mum most of the time, holding her hand, gently stroking it. I remember hearing what seemed to be the distant sound of an ambulance siren and realising that it was coming from the one we were in, and yet from the outside, they always sounded so loud. It was different being on the inside. I felt like we were in a bubble, was this really happening? Looking around at all the equipment. I couldn't see out of the windows because they were tinted, and it was still dark outside. I was amazed at how fast the ambulance was going. At one stage, I remember thinking, when we took a bend so sharply, just as well my mum is strapped in, or she would have fallen off the bed. I didn't know they went so fast, yet at the same time, I felt we were in safe hands with the very experienced driver.

Even though they were two strangers, I felt very secure with them, and I knew my mum was also. I leaned forward to look out of the front windscreen to see where we were, but all I could see were lots of red brake lights of the cars stopping in front of us. It was now morning rush hour. They are stepping aside for us to get through, I thought. I have stepped aside for many ambulances, as drivers do, and we always prayed for the situation when one was passing. I wonder if anyone was praying for us. Now the cars are stepping aside for us. I kept praying and praying from the bottom of my heart, for Jesus is our only hope. Who else can we turn to? There is no one else who has the power to intervene like Jesus. No one else has the divine connection to know and to see into our hearts, minds and situations. He is our only refuge. How sad I felt to see my mum, who was always so strong and in control, lying there so vulnerable. Where is she going, being sucked into a vacuum? I know she believes in God, but she didn't go to Church, and what really is her relationship with Him? Could she go somewhere other than Heaven? Not Hell, please God. I thought about some of the Sermons I have heard, "If you don't believe in Jesus and are not saved, you will go to Hell". Please don't let her go, God. I wanted to pick her up and cuddle her in my arms and say everything is going to be all right, mum. I prayed that God would heal her and give her another chance, and us as a family, and I prayed that Jesus would please give her a divine encounter with Him so that she would have an opportunity to really know Him for real, just like He has done for so many other people, including myself. She has always believed in God and is quite a "reserved" Christian, although she does not go to Church regularly. My prayer was, **"Jesus, please give her an encounter with you to know you are real".** As I was praying, surrendering to God, and looking at my mum, I suddenly felt a

powerful divine presence in the ambulance, and it seemed to be above her and all over her. It was so strong and tangible. I felt such a rush of excitement going through my whole body. I just knew the Presence of God was covering her. I could describe it as a hovering blanket of power or mist, but it seems far too Holy to describe it in such a way. However, I have since heard of other peoples Angel encounters who have said the same thing, a blanket of power. All of a sudden, her hands began to shake, not twist anymore, but gently flutter, and I recognised it to be just like when The Holy Spirit touches people. I get it in my right hand when I pray and worship our Lord Jesus, so I knew the gentleness of the shaking in her hands. I am excited again, just writing this. The ambulance was full of the powerful presence of God.

Suddenly, there was an instant change in her eyes, and she became calm as if her breath had just returned to her. I just knew that God had touched her. She seemed to just totally relax, like after a big gasp. Then she seemed very calm, and the look of fear had gone from her face. I just knew something divine had taken place. There was a peaceful quietness; it seemed that time itself had stopped, similar to when watching a film and it freezes, or you put it on pause. Even the paramedic was quiet and still. I was very aware that something amazing was happening, and yet there was stillness and excitement at the same time. I could maybe describe it as when you walk into a room where you are reuniting with an old friend or someone very special, and you can sense their presence in the room, you know they are already there, and you get that rush of excitement, but haven't actually seen them yet. A bit like that feeling, but 100 times more. The ambulance was full of the presence of God. My mother then calmly spoke, gently asking why we didn't go to the other hospital, which was the one we usually would use.

She hadn't heard the paramedics discussing the hospital with me at the bungalow as we were not in the same room but in the hallway at the time. It didn't really hit me that she had actually spoken clearly, or the paramedic for that matter, but we both answered her. What a wonderful privilege it had been to be in the presence of a divine encounter, to witness an actual Miracle.

Within seconds of her speaking, we arrived at the hospital; the doors of the ambulance burst open, and the driver and the paramedic in the back with us rushed my mum into Accident & Emergency. I stood around for a few minutes looking to see if my dad and sister had arrived as yet, and suddenly noticed that the other lady paramedic, who was at the house and had the mop of strawberry-ginger hair, had followed the ambulance in her car. I hadn't realised that she was coming, because I said goodbye and thanked her earlier when we left. It was such a lovely, comforting surprise to see her. She said she wasn't busy, so she came along. I hugged her and thanked her again. I felt so pleased that she would even think about coming with us. How blessed we were. I followed the paramedic to A&E, and she went in with the others while I stood outside the room where they had taken my mum.

Within a few minutes, the paramedic who was sitting in the back of the ambulance with us walked out of the room shaking his head, saying, "I cant' believe it; your mum is talking." I smiled, and my face must have lit up. "That's the power of Prayer." I replied. "It's something." He said, nodding his head in almost disbelief because he knew that something very unusual had happened. Then, a few minutes later, the lady paramedic who followed us in her car came out of the room my mum was in and said, "I can't believe it; your mum is sitting up talking." "I know." I replied. The paramedics certainly know an emergency when they see one, and they knew this was an extremely serious situation from the start. For them to actually say they couldn't believe it, I knew, anyway, that we had just experienced a true divine **Miracle from God**. I looked around to see that my dad and sister had arrived; my dad's head was looking down at the floor with sadness. I rushed up to them and told them that she was sitting up talking and what had happened in the ambulance. My dad knew instantly it was God and shook his head, smiling in amazement through his sad eyes.

They eventually let us go into the room to see my mum. I can't explain or put into words just how it felt to be able to communicate with her again. I hugged her and told her that God had touched her in the ambulance, and then she began to cry. I was so pleased to be able to ask her and find out exactly what she was thinking. We had been given another chance. I am so thankful to our Lord Jesus. He answered our prayers. He is so kind, loving and faithful.

With total exhilaration, I wanted to know everything, every detail. Although, at the time, I had no idea of what actually took place in the ambulance, I just knew that God was there and Jesus had healed her instantly. We were both so excited, hugging each other and overflowing with joy and excitement. She said she was not afraid; she was just wondering how she was going to get my dad's attention. She said she got up to go to the toilet and fell into the small room. As she tried to get up, she accidentally kicked the door, and then it closed. She said she couldn't move on the floor. She heard, was aware of, and remembered everything, every detail that was going on. She told me that when she was on the floor, she thought she was speaking in tongues; she knew it was another language, not French or German, but a language with some long words, which she was trying to work out; it wasn't babble, but actual words, another language. It was unusual for my mum to say this because she had not spoken in tongues before; she had heard about it but didn't know very much about it. They didn't speak in tongues in the Church of England that we knew. They do in the Pentecostal church that I go to, but she hadn't come with me to that church then. She didn't get it confused with the noises she was making. She was aware of not being able to communicate. My mum is a very practical person, and if she was unsure about anything, she would definitely not say it.

My mum's blood pressure was very high, and her heart rate was irregular, which was not surprising considering the shock her body had just been through. She suffered from high blood pressure anyway. She remembered everything, every detail. I stood next to her while she was on the bed, holding her hand and saying that she had a Miracle in the ambulance. We sat there, and she began to feel such joy and then started to laugh like an excited little child. I had not seen her like this for a very long time. We were laughing together, and the Joy of the Lord was all over her. People were looking at us. I kept saying to her that God touched her in the ambulance. (Even at this time, we both had not realised the extent of what had actually happened in the ambulance).

By the time the Doctor came to see her, which was quite a while later, he asked her questions about dates, birthdays, and counting backwards, and she passed all the tests. He asked her to say funny words, like octopus. Her face was back to normal as well. The drop had also gone. He didn't even think she was showing signs of a stroke. I think he thought we were playing a game, wasting his time, and he didn't seem very impressed because my mum was laughing and full of joy, and he said he was going to release her when they got her blood pressure down. I could tell the doctor thought it was not much to be concerned about, and he had not seen her earlier anyway, so he was only going on what he was seeing now. I wanted the doctor to know that in the morning, just a few hours before, she was not at all like this and just how serious it was. I guess in the back of my mind, I was worried in case it happened again, and I know that I shouldn't have really had any doubting thoughts because of her Miracle, but I wanted to doctor to know what had happened. Then, while she was speaking, her speech suddenly slurred a little. I wonder now, looking back, if God allowed this, because had it not, they would not have done a brain scan. I think I just wanted to prove to everyone that she had had a Miracle, although I didn't have to because the proof was already there. Only the Paramedics, my mum and dad, my sister and I, and Jesus, God, the Holy Spirit and the Angels, of course, knew and saw her as she was in the morning. Then the doctor said he would do a brain scan, so we waited around. I spoke to my mum, telling her again that God had touched her and healed her. She felt so pleased and very special. There suddenly seemed to be a very strong bond between us, which was very powerful. **Again, we both did not know what actually had happened in the ambulance at this point.**

Later, the scan results showed no sign of a stroke. Well, of course, it wouldn't; a Miracle had taken place before the brain scan. They kept her in the hospital because they thought it might be other things, like a blockage of an artery in the neck and did other checks, but the test results all came back clear. She was doing very well, sitting up, chatting a lot, and very, very happy.

Unfortunately, while she was in the hospital, she caught a bug, sickness, diarrhoea and cramps in her legs. We thought it might be the medication for the heart rate that they gave her or the food she had eaten, but apparently, there was a bug going around that a few patients in the hospital had, but the hospital didn't want to make a big thing about it. It was in the newspapers, called "The Winter Bug", and all the symptoms of it were what she had. I must admit, I did wonder what was going on, and I kept praying and claiming the promises of God in His Scriptures. The family were worried, but I knew God had given her a Miracle, and He would not let us down now. We had to keep trusting in Him. My son told me, "Nannie will be all right and will be home soon". The true faith of a child.

Chapter 13

The Miracle Revealed

My parents celebrated their Diamond Wedding Anniversary while my mum was in the hospital. We took in some cake and balloons. She was in for 10 days in the end. A couple of days before she came out, I went to visit her and sat beside her; my dad was also there. I hadn't had a chance to speak to her before that because they closed the ward to visitors due to the bug, and then when she got over that, there were many other family members visiting her. My dad bought her a diamond ring for their anniversary, which we helped him choose at the jeweller while she was in the hospital, and he gave it to her. For once, my dad didn't mind spending on her; he knew that he had almost lost her, so he realised that money didn't mean anything to him, although the ring wasn't too expensive, but definitely a lot more than he would have even thought about spending before.

As I was saying, it was a couple of days before she came out of the hospital; my dad and I were her only visitors for a change, so we had time to speak to her and catch up. I kept on about the touch from Jesus in the ambulance, telling her how special and privileged she was. She was very happy and asked me, "Who have you told?" "**Everyone!**" I replied. And I had because I just knew it was Jesus who had done it, and I wanted Him to be glorified. It wouldn't have been what it was without Him, so I couldn't tell it any other way. How could I tell what had happened to my mum without mentioning the main part, her Miracle! I thank, of course, the work of the NHS doctors and nurses, the ambulance paramedics and the team, and I do not take away the excellent help they gave, but I was so excited about what God had done; I felt His divine presence, His Holy Spirit and felt so privileged to be part of it. Anyway, as we were chatting, I asked her again if she remembered anything unusual. I wanted to know exactly what happened in the ambulance, every detail of what she saw because I knew something amazing had taken place.

She casually said, "Not really..." and began to speak about the three paramedics in the ambulance and the one at the bungalow, and that she wanted to find out their names and give them all some chocolates, to thank them personally. I was puzzled, as there weren't three paramedics in the ambulance, and I said to her that there were only two paramedics in the ambulance, the driver and the paramedic who was in the back with me. She said, yes, the driver and the man in the back, but there was also a tall lady who stepped in just before the doors closed. I asked her if she meant the paramedic who had arrived earlier in the car, who saw her first, with the strawberry-ginger hair. She insisted it was not her; she remembered what she looked like and remembered her saying goodbye to us at the door of the ambulance and also asking if we wanted her to take my dad to the hospital. My mum said this was a tall lady, who stepped into the ambulance, and after she stepped in, the doors closed behind her. She was dressed as a paramedic. She said that I was already sitting in the single seat at the back, with the seatbelt around me that the other paramedic had clipped in, and my mum remembered me waving at her. He then sat beside her bed, and she remembers everything he was saying, and there was the driver; of course, she mentioned him too. I tested my mum again to see if she had got confused with the other lady paramedic who was there earlier, but she had remembered everything so clearly, even the colour of her hair and that she was totally different to the one who stepped into the ambulance. There was not one thing she said that had not happened. She actually remembered things I had forgotten! My mum even knew the route we took to the hospital, which I hadn't a clue about because you can't see out of the windows. She was very accurate in every detail. I told her that there wasn't another lady paramedic in the ambulance with us. My mum looked shocked.

My mum said that this lady had stepped into the ambulance with her head down. She was very tall with straight white blonde hair to her shoulders. Then the doors closed, and she moved and stood behind the paramedic, who was sitting next to her bed. I said I didn't think there was enough room to stand there. My mum said the lady then moved and stood between the paramedic and me, and then she moved forward and stood over her (which is where I felt the very strong Power and Presence of God), and my mum said the lady blocked me out of view. She said the lady was doing something with the equipment above her, which looked like the old-fashioned Bakelite switches, and then she said to her, "**Don't worry, you will be all right**". My mum said that she almost spoke back to the lady, then she saw that she had a beautiful light, like a large golden/orange crystal diamond, in her hand. I do get so excited every time I think about this. She said it was a very bright light, and she was admiring how beautiful it was, and then the light seemed to be getting brighter and brighter and suddenly so very bright that she couldn't look at it anymore, and she shook her head, and when she did, the light was easier to see and was more crystallised, and not as bright. I think that was the point when I noticed the change in my mum's eyes. Not that I knew or saw what was going on, but I knew something miraculous had happened by the look on her face.

My mum said she thought it was funny because the lady was not strapped in or holding on, the ambulance was going all over the place, and she had not fallen over or stumbled. She said at one point; she thought the lady would fall on her as she was standing over her because the ambulance took such a sharp turn. (That was the one I told you about earlier when I said if my mum wasn't strapped in, she would have fallen off the bed). And then we both smiled. I said, "Mum, God sent an Angel. It was an Angel. I knew God gave you a Miracle".

She said again that the Angel was tall and had very fair blonde, almost white hair down to her shoulders. She didn't see her face, just the sides of her hair. What excites me so much is that the presence of God is so powerful, and I am so privileged to have recognised it. Had I not kept on about it, people would be none the wiser, not realising that my mum had an Angel from God sent to minister to her in the ambulance, and she would have just taken it for granted that there were three of us there with her and that the Angel was just another paramedic.

My mum said that at one time in the ambulance, she felt like she was very high up, and she heard a funny humming noise, like being in an aeroplane. I wonder if this was when I felt that she was going high up into a vacuum. I know reading this, some people may think that my mum has had some sort of a time-lapse with the lady paramedics and perhaps got confused, but if you know my mum, the fact that she remembers every detail of the whole time, even in the hospital, and even the state her mind was supposedly in at home on the floor, my mum knows 100 per cent that the two lady paramedics were two totally different people. I kept testing my mum to see if she was confused, but the fact that she insisted that the lady was there in the ambulance when it was moving, I know physically there was only the paramedic, my mum and myself in the back. And I have questioned my own sanity! Also, I have since been told that an ambulance doesn't take three people in the back. If a relative goes in the ambulance with the patient, then there will be one other paramedic in the back. But if there is no relative going, then there will be two paramedics in the back with the patient. My mum saw three of us in the back, one was me, of course, but the other paramedic was the driver.

Needless to say, my mum and I spent many precious times recalling the wonderful Miracle of God. We loved to talk about it and go over every detail, and each time we did, something more was revealed.

She has since told me that at the time in the bedroom when she was on the floor when it first happened, she felt the face of God above her to the right, and she spoke with Him, asking whether she should go or not, and she thought of all her family and felt she should stay because it would obviously be such a shock for everyone. She said she asked God not to take her yet, as it is not how she wanted to be found. This is what I mean when I say that we know not what goes on with people in their time of need, whether they believe in God or not, but if He is there at the end of their lives, then they cannot deny it. They may naturally connect with God anyway. I would never have known that if I hadn't been able to speak to my mum again. She also said someone else was there to meet her in the bedroom, someone she knew, ready to take her.

One of the most amazing things about all of this I found is that my mum and I were in the same dimension, yet she could see me and the Angel at the same time, so all three of us were in the same dimension, and the Angel must have been able to see me as well. I could sense the presence of God, but I didn't see the Angel, and I knew 100 per cent that God was there healing my mum. And I find it amazing that my mum said the Angel actually blocked me out when she stood in front of me, leaning over my mum, so she was in the same dimension as me and yet I couldn't see her, only feel the presence. And all the time, the paramedic was quiet and still; he had no idea what was going on. Can time stand still? In the Bible, it mentions that Joshua prayed to the Lord in front of all the people of Israel "Let the sun stand still over Gibeon and the moon over the valley of Aijalon". So the sun stood still, and the moon stayed in place until the nation of Israel had defeated its enemies. Joshua 10:12-13. Joshua commanded the sun and the moon to stand still so that he and his army might continue fighting by daylight. So time stood still in the Bible. God heard Joshua's prayer and gave him a Miracle.

My mum and I now have a wonderfully close relationship, and we keep talking about it every time we see each other. We were not so close before this happened. We are so connected now. Some people seem sceptical, or are in disbelief about what happened, or really don't understand it, but it doesn't matter because we know what happened; we were there. Even the paramedics knew there was a Miracle, but they didn't realise to what extent or what actually happened. God sent an Angel on a mission to bring a Miracle for my mum.

Even the pure white cotton wool ball that the nurse taped to my mum's arm after her blood test when we removed it had a perfect bright red heart shape on it. As the photo shows:

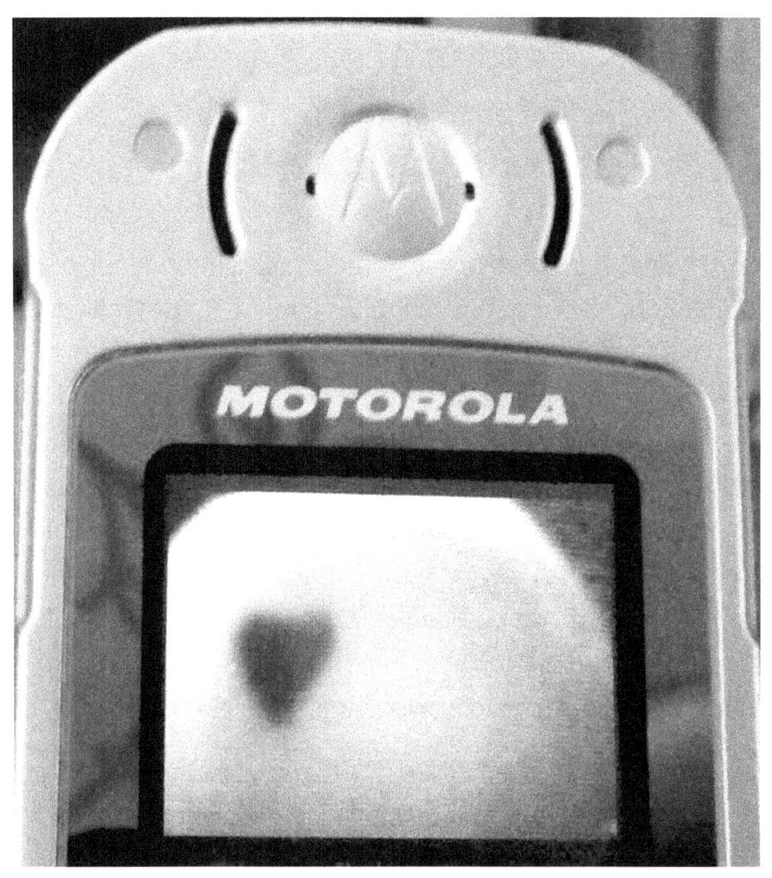

My son believes in Miracles, we have seen quite a few of them, and he knew without a doubt that all was ok. He has a lot of faith as well. I was telling everyone. What a privilege to be part of it and witness it; I thank God for giving me the blessing to be there. And as my mum said, had I not gone on about it so much, she would have just thought it was another paramedic in the ambulance telling her that everything would be all right. How funny that she didn't even think of it all until after we spoke about it, how it all comes together.

Chapter 14

God chose us

I just want to say when we wonder and doubt about our loved ones salvation, the scripture comes to mind that "God gives His Angels charge over us to protect us…" (Psalm 91) and, "Are they not all ministering spirits, sent forth to minister to those who will inherit salvation?" (Hebrews 1 v 14 NKJV.) I know Angles exist, and we should not pray to them, but only to our lovely Jesus Christ, but it is written so clearly for us to see and believe they are here for us to help us in our times of need. And just how many times have people literally "entertained Angels" without knowing it. The Bible even says so "Do not forget to entertain strangers, for by so doing some have unwittingly entertained angels." (Hebrews 13 v.2).

Also, it made me realise how we worry about our loved ones. If God has chosen them to be His saints, He will save them. He says in His Word, "Long ago, even before He made the world, God loved us and chose us in Christ to be holy and without fault in His eyes." (Eph 1- v.4-9). "Furthermore, because of Christ, we have received an inheritance from God, for He chose us from the beginning and all things happen just as He decided long ago". (Eph. 1. 11).

"It is God who saved us and chose us to live a holy life. He did this not because we deserved it, but because that was His plan long ago before the world began, to show his love and kindness to us through Christ Jesus. (2 Timothy 1:9). Look at the criminal on the cross next to Jesus; he said, "Jesus, remember me when you come into your kingdom." (Luke 23:42) And Jesus replied, "Assuredly, I say to you, today you will be with Me in paradise." (Luke 23:43). The criminal turned to Jesus, in the very last hours of his life. And what a privilege to actually be with Jesus in the flesh, the only one who has power over death. He is still the same Yesterday, Today and Forever, and He will look after us. We need not concern ourselves that we have not prayed properly or said the right thing or our prayers are not long enough. God hears our hearts, the cries of our hearts. There is power in the name of Jesus. Just by calling His name. "Behold, I stand at the door and knock, if anyone hears My voice, and opens the door, I will come in to him and dine with him, and he with Me" (Revelation 3:20). "For whosoever shall call upon the name of the Lord shall be saved". Romans (10.v:13). Jesus wants to save every one of us. "What do you think? Suppose a man has a hundred sheep. If one of them strays, does he not leave the other ninety-nine on the hillside and go in search of the one that strayed? And if he should find it, I tell you this; he is more delighted over that sheep than over the ninety-nine that never strayed. In the same way, it is not your heavenly Father's will that one of these little ones should be lost". (Matthew 18.v:12.)

There may be many people who have not had the opportunity to speak to loved ones again or are wondering what happened to them. It is not our place to judge, and many have been put into misery by, I am afraid to say, some people in the church, who judge who they claim to be "unsaved loved ones" when they do not know their hearts and minds, and they tell people that their relatives have gone to hell. This leaves them in spiritual bondage and can sometimes have the reverse effect and completely put people off the church. Who can blame them. I have actually heard it said in church. Only God Himself is the Judge, and we cannot claim to know the extent of the heart and mind of God and what He decides to do. Even Jesus said when James and John asked Him if they could sit on either side of Him in Heaven, "But I have no right to say who will sit on my right or my left. God has prepared those places for the ones He has chosen." (Mark 10.40 NLT). If I hadn't been able to communicate again with my mum, I guess I would be wondering too, because of what other people had said, even though she is a Christian. She didn't go to Church every Sunday. She prays and speaks to God but doesn't read her Bible every night, and yet, a breath away from death, God gave her a Miracle. God loves all of us. I am not trying to make things look as though we should sail through life without acknowledging Jesus and that we will be all right in the end. He knows our hearts and minds, and of course, we need to receive Him as our Lord and Saviour, who He is, so that we may have eternal life. He gave His life for us, overcame death on the cross, and was resurrected. He came to take away the fear of death, which was put into the world by the devil, by overcoming it and showing we can live again. "That though death He might destroy him that had the power of death, that is, the devil, and deliver them who through fear of death were all their lifetime subject to bondage." (Hebrews 2 v14-15. KJV). "Because God's children are human beings - made of flesh and blood - Jesus also became flesh and blood by being born in human form for only as a human being could he die, and only by dying could He break the power of the devil who had power over death. Only in this way could He deliver those who have lived all their lives as slaves to the fear of dying. " (Heb. 2 v.14 -15).

I sometimes wonder, most of us fear death if we are honest, but it was the devil who put the fear there. None of us knows what death is like unless we have experienced it. There are many, of course, who have died and been able to come back to tell what they experienced, but there is no one I have ever heard of who can tell us what being born (in the flesh) is like. A new born baby can't tell another baby in the hospital what they have just been through, and being born is not something we seem to remember. Some people can remember way back to being a toddler or even being a baby, but I don't know of anyone who can remember their birth. Imagine knowing beforehand, if you were told, ok, you are going to start off as a cell the size of a seed, grow and take shape in a bag of water for about 9 months in somebody else's body, and then be squeezed out into the open world. Not many would fancy the idea, but we have all experienced it. It just as well we didn't know beforehand; otherwise, not many of us would want to do it, especially if you are claustrophobic like I am, but look beyond that, a beautifully created world full of flowers, life, love, happiness, laughter, and a few ups and downs, of course. Anyway, it's not so bad, is it, for some of us. I think the same about death, we fear it, yet Jesus tells us what an amazing future we have in Heaven, no more sickness, no more disease, no tears, no night-time and no more death. And that is how we can live together for eternity if we accept Jesus Christ as our Lord and Saviour and believe that He is the Son of God, who gave His life for us on the cross to save mankind. And it is that simple. He does not complicate things as we do. Jesus said, "Most assuredly, I say to you, he who believes in Me has everlasting life" (John 6:47); some people never get the opportunity to know how God met with their loved ones at their time to leave this world and may spend years worrying for nothing. As I said above, think about the thief on the cross next to Jesus. He called to Jesus, and Jesus told him, "Today you will be with me in paradise". The thief knew he was a sinner, but at the end of his life, he certainly knew who Jesus was. He doesn't want any of us to perish but all to be saved. Who knows what goes on in the heart and mind of someone in their last minutes on earth. And one thing I am sure of now, God sends His Angels to us so we are never alone, and where we cannot do anymore for the loved ones that have departed, we know that God's Angels are there to pick up where we left off, and carry them to Heaven.

Chapter 15

Power in the Name of Jesus

Some people do not believe that Jesus heals today and say that healing was only for the time when Jesus was on earth with His disciples. I can say first hand that I have been healed myself more than once, and I know of and have seen many other people who have been healed. Jesus Christ is the same yesterday, today and forever, and He wants to heal us today.

Needless to say, my mum felt so blessed. Her Miracle has totally changed her as a person. She realises that I am not "quite so mad" after all and how privileged she is to be healed by Almighty God Himself through Jesus Christ, who came for all of us. And He really does "give His Angels charge over us to protect us wherever we go." (Psalm 91). The hospital did think she had a stroke, by all the symptoms that were recorded by the paramedics, although it didn't make sense to them because there was no sign of it on the scan.

As I said, my mum used to be on a lot of medication. Some of the tablets she was on made her feel weak after coming out of the hospital. The funny thing is, at the time she had her Miracle healing from Jesus, I thought to myself, she doesn't need all this medication she is on because she has been healed. I prayed that if that was the case, Jesus would sort it out and reveal it. My mum has been on tablets most of her life and was very dependent on them in the past for migraine and other things. She actually asked the doctor and the consultant at the hospital to take her off some of her medication; she said that she didn't need them, and they were making her feel worse.

She suffered from the side effects of some of the tablets, which were referred to in the leaflet. In fact, one of the doctors that she saw told her that she was a walking pharmacy, that she didn't need all the medication she was one. She came off a lot of the medication and never felt so good and was happy doing all the things she used to do before and more.

Everything to do with this has been special. Even the Consultant at the hospital sent a letter to her Doctor saying to "look after this patient." He knew something special had taken place. The ball of cotton wool that they put on her arm after she had a blood test showed a very clear red heart shape on it. When God is with us, He will provide the very best. Amen.

I just wanted to share this with you. Almost every day, I share it with someone, and it gives so much hope to people. Especially coming from someone like my mum, who has to literally "See it to believe it." We can all think of many times in our lives when we have had divine help in many situations. Sometimes, it's not until you sit back and think over the whole situation you realise that what happened doesn't always make sense, and little things come to you later because, at the time, so much is going on that you can't take it all in.

There are many testimonies of people's divine encounters, and I love to hear and read about them. Some unbelieving and also believing people say, "If so-and-so is miraculously healed, then I will believe". When they see that "so-and-so" has been miraculously healed, they still don't believe the Miracle. It can be hard to believe a Miracle until it happens to you. Then try explaining it to others. Jesus did many Miracles in the Bible. Most of His ministry was casting out demons from people, healing the sick and lame, and even raising the dead. The Pharisees, the religious leaders, rejected Jesus' Miracles, especially when Jesus healed the demon-possessed man and everyone was amazed. When the Pharisees heard this, they blasphemed, saying, "It is only by Beelzebub, the prince of demons, that this fellow drives out demons". (Matthew 12:24). Jesus knew their thoughts and said to them, "Every kingdom divided against itself is brought to desolation; and every city or house divided against itself shall not stand: And if Satan cast out Satan, he is divided against himself; how shall then his kingdom stand. And if I by Beelzebub cast out devils, by whom do your children cast them out? Therefore they shall be your judges. But if I cast out devils **by the Spirit of God**, then the **kingdom of God is come unto you**." (Matthew 12:25-28 KJV). I love the answers Jesus gives in the Bible and how He deals with everything.

Jesus gave His disciples "power against unclean spirits, to cast them out, and to heal all manner of sickness and all manner of disease." (Matthew 10:v1 KJV).

Jesus told His disciples before He ascended to Heaven, "All power is given unto me in Heaven and in earth. Go ye therefore, and teach all nations, baptising them in the name of the Father, and of the Son and of the Holy Spirit; Teaching them to observe all things whatsoever I have commanded you; **and, lo, I am with you always, even unto the end of the world."** Amen. (Matthew 28:v 17-20 KJV.) What an amazing gift to have Jesus with us always.

"God worked unusual miracles by the hands of Paul so that even handkerchiefs or aprons were brought from his body to the sick, and the diseases left them and the evil spirits went out of them." (Acts 19:11-12 NKJV). Paul had authority over evil spirits, and when he was in Ephesus, there were many magicians and people practising witchcraft there. When they saw the power Paul had in the name of Jesus to cast out demons and heal the sick, many of them turned to Christ.

Chapter 16

Our Saviour's Prayer

If we open our hearts to the Lord Jesus Christ, we will truly see wonderful, miraculous things. He will be with you all the time and wants to be your best friend. You will see just how real He is. Just look to Him. Why wait until later, people who don't know Him all their lives have missed out on so much. Their lives could have been so much more beautifully fulfilled, fruitful, and full of love and blessings, more than they could ever have imagined. They could have dealt with the hard times in such a different way, having the Holy One to comfort and be with them, to advise them and help them. I used to have so much faith I would drive along in the car talking to Jesus, my best friend, not only in the car but everywhere. I asked His advice, prayed about jobs and situations, and have seen miraculous things happen. I cannot imagine life without Jesus Christ. I don't say there haven't been hard times, but without Jesus, they would have been impossible to get through. I tell some people who say there is no God, well, if I were a non-believer, I would rather take a chance and believe there could be rather than miss out on eternal life. For what have they got to lose, if there is nothing, then we are none the wiser. But there is a whole lot to lose if you believe in nothing, and there is eternal life in Heaven to gain just by believing in Jesus Christ. "That if thou shalt confess with thy mouth the Lord Jesus, and shall believe in thine heart that God hath raised Him from the dead thou shalt be saved". (Romans 10:9) "For whosoever shall call upon the name of the Lord shall be saved." (Romans 10:13)

Please pray this prayer with me if you want Jesus Christ to come into your life and you haven't already invited Him to. I know your life will be blessed.

> *I believe Jesus Christ is the Son of God,*
> *who died for me, to set me free.*
> *Please come into my heart, and live with me,*
> *and keep me with you, eternally.*
> *I love you Lord Jesus. Amen.*

Now you belong to the family of God. Hello and welcome, my brothers and sisters. He knew you were going to say this prayer a long time ago; remember the scripture above. He knew you before the world began. He has just been waiting for you. Now you will be telling others, like I have, about the wonderful things Jesus Christ has done for you and your loved ones. Your lives will never be the same. Read the Bible. It is God's Written Manual for Life. Everything you need to know for every situation is in there, and much much more. Watch Biblical films about Jesus or watch the Bible word for word online, and get to know Jesus Christ as your closest best friend. There is a wonderful way of reading the Bible online, it's called The WatchWord Bible, and you can watch it on YouTube. It has the scriptures on the screen while showing the film in the background, so it is easy to understand.

And to you brothers and sisters who are already in Christ, keep talking about the wonderful things God has done and is doing in your lives. We are here to spread the Good News of Jesus Christ, our Lord, and Saviour. To Him be all the glory.

My mum and I loved to talk about her Testimony whenever we could. It is still as fresh as the day it happened and as special as ever. Every time we see an ambulance, I still pray for the situation and remember that wonderful day when God intervened for us, and I wonder if there is an Angel on board. In a world where there is so much going on, so much suffering and hopelessness, look up, and there you will see our wonderful Saviour waiting for you with His arms wide open.

Love and God Bless you all

Chapter 17

Church Without Walls

It never fails; I put on the music, mum and dad's music, and there I am, back in the moment. Connie Francis, my mum, singing along to "My Heart has a mind of its own". I can see her now singing and dancing along to it. My dad holding her and dancing around the front room together, playing their 45s and LPs, Jim Reeves, Doris day. Or just sitting in their chairs listening to music.

Every Saturday, the family would meet up at my mum and dad's, and there would always be food on the go. Usually a curry and chapatis, dhal and rice. We would walk into the pair of them in the kitchen, chopping onions and rolling out atta. Jim Reeves would be playing loud in the other room, or Charlie Pride. One of my dad's favourite snacks was peanut butter on toast; better still, he would put it back under the grill with the peanut butter on it, and the whole house would smell of roasted peanuts, and it was the best smell and taste ever. The recipe was simple, make your toast, add your butter and a nice thick coat of peanut butter, put it back under the grill and wait for the peanut butter to bubble up a bit, but not too much, and you definitely needed to leave it to cool for a few minutes; otherwise that hot peanut butter would stick to the roof of your mouth, and you wouldn't be able to taste anything for a day or two. I can highly recommend it, and if you are even more adventurous, put some sliced banana on the sizzling peanut toast. My dad called it "Peanut Butter Baked Toast". We loved it. You can't put it in the toaster, though, as someone once did; it has to go under the grill.

Everyone was welcome. Many times friends would pop in, and it would eventually end up as a party or a large gathering.

Back in the 60s and 70s, my mum and dad had parties almost every weekend; if it wasn't at their house, it would be one of their many friends hosting it. They took turns. A lot of their friends had also come to the UK from India, and they all kept in touch, even though they lived distances away from each other. Everyone had such a good time. The kids would be playing in another room while the adults danced, drank and got very merry.

I remember the next morning after the parties, at our home, my sister and I would help to clean up, picking up the nuts and crisps that were left lying around, we spent most of the day cleaning up, and the windows would be wide open releasing the lingering smell of cigars and whisky from the night before.

It was nice to see the other side of my parents, relaxed and joking with their friends, having a break from being strict with us.

One of my mum's brothers lived in Yorkshire, and he had a large family, and we would go and spend time with them, and the kids would again play outside and have fun. Her other brother and his family lived in New Zealand. They would come and stay with us when they came to the UK.

Most of my dad's family were still in India, apart from one of his brothers, who lived in North London, and again we would all meet up often, having great times. Eventually, the families got so big we would have to arrange to meet up on mutual ground and hire a hall or meet in a park in the summer for a picnic. When we got together as time went on, the young children in our families grew up, and they became the ones who were arranging everything, whilst our parents sat back and slowed down, drinking tea and chatting in the comfy chairs as the next generation moved forward. My cousins would arrange games when we got together, and as we were from South London and they were from North London, we would have games competitions North v South. The brother-in-laws from the South were a good team, but the North London boys took some beating. There was the odd tie, but mainly the North won. They were really good days. When you look at the legacies, our parents leave behind.

♥

My mum loved to watch meaningful programmes, like how things are made and historical programmes. She was so interested in the world around us and was full of wisdom and knowledge. She was very sharp and didn't miss a thing.

When we were young, I remember she would often take cuttings of plants when we went out to a restaurant or a friend's house and wrap the smallest cuttings into her handkerchief. Within weeks the cuttings would be sprouting on her kitchen windowsill, which eventually was planted and grew into large healthy plants. She was so good at everything she put her hands on. She loved her garden in her younger days. I think she could totally feel at home with nature there and away from everything. Everything she did was done to perfection. She would spend hours in her garden, painting stones and ornaments and cutting back her beautiful roses, which are still thriving today.

She was always very slim and looked beautifully groomed. She would put her rollers in after she washed her hair. I remember the tiny rollers she had and the sponge ones. There were the pink and blue plastic ones, which she would push the hairpins into to hold them in; they always looked so tight, as if they were pulling her hair. Then she would take them out, and I would sit beside her, gathering the pins and putting them into the place she had designated for them. Everything had its place. Then she would brush her lovely dark brown hair, and it looked perfect. She only used face powder and red lipstick. I never saw her use any creams; she said she didn't like the feel of cream on her skin, only soap and water, and yet she had beautiful soft skin, which didn't start to age until she was in her 80s. The odd wrinkle but nothing to worry about.

♥

After her Miracle, and like I said, it totally changed her; my mum and dad would take communion together on a Sunday in their living room. They would turn the TV on at 10.30 every Sunday to Revelation TV, a wonderful Christian channel, and watch a programme called "Church Without Walls". It was such a lovely programme for people who couldn't get to Church or for anyone who didn't actually go to Church but could participate. They would get out their best crystal glasses and either cherryaid or blackcurrant squash and bread and take communion together. I would join in with them if I was there, but they still did it together on their own, which was so wonderful to see.

My parents were great with all their grandchildren, and they were far more tolerant grandparents than they were parents.

On their 65th wedding anniversary, we arranged a meal at a local Indian restaurant with some of the family and a few of their friends. We took a Jim Reeves CD and asked them to play one of the tracks, which was one of their favourites and happened to be the first track on the CD. When it came on, faces in the restaurant lit up, and they started singing along too. They loved it. I think many people related to it, reminding them of their parents listening to it and bringing back memories for them. The manager let the whole CD play, and it was very nice.

Also, hearing all the stories that our parents told us when we were younger didn't seem to mean much to us then. Oh, that story again. And when you listen to people as they get older, wanting to know their ancestors, you think it's an age thing, and you say to yourself that maybe one day I will get around to doing that. Ask while you have the time because one day, there will be no parents to answer the questions. And you don't have any answers to the questions anymore. You wished that you had made notes or listened.

Chapter 18

I have overcome the World

Like most teenagers, growing up, I went through a stage of questioning and really needing answers to the world we live in. I never once doubted my faith in Jesus Christ, and I never blamed God for the things going on in the world because I knew there was an enemy of God, who was out cause as much destruction as possible, yet poor God was always blamed. I used to pray about something and then open my Bible, and God would always give me an answer using His Word. I would love to read the Psalms and Proverbs. I loved to read the words Jesus spoke, which were written in red in the Bible. When I was younger, the Old Testament seemed quite boring to me, but as I have gotten older, I really love to hear about the prophets in the Bible. They were no different to us, and I love to read about the things they did and went through.

My relationship with Jesus was so strong that I knew He would always be with me, as He promised in His Word. I trusted Him with everything then, and I do now and always will. He said in His Word, "These things I have spoken to you, that in Me you may have peace. In the world you will have tribulation'; but be of good cheer, I have overcome the world." (John 15:33 NKJV). I couldn't think of anything better than having the One who overcame the world as my personal friend and saviour and that He is actually here for you and me and all of us. I feel that I have finally come to a place of peace in my heart and mind. Jesus gives us peace that passes all understanding. I also feel wiser too, because I have matured in my faith through the trials of life and, of course, in my years on earth. It didn't happen overnight, and some people only like to remind you of your failures or difficult times, and growing up, I had a few, as many people do. Wouldn't it be wonderful if we had this wisdom when we were young, we would miss all the difficult bits; but learning is all part of life's journey. Although I have always had very strong faith, I was still young in faith and in the world. The Bible talks about a time of spiritual immaturity, God understands we need to grow, but once we have, we shouldn't go backwards because we know the Truth. "For though by this time you ought to be teachers, you need someone to teach you again the first principles of the oracles of God, and you have come to need milk and not solid food. For everyone who partakes only of milk is unskilled in the word of righteousness, for he is a babe. But solid food belongs to those who are of full age; this is, those who by reasons of use have their senses exercised to discern both good and evil." (Hebrews 5:12-14). But it's not easy. As much faith as you have, when trials are unbearable, it is sometimes easy to want milk because you don't want to face the reality of what is going on around you, but it is even better when you can stand up strong in faith and say that you are going to overcome this battle, as you have done all the others, and come out stronger every time, and you are not going to doubt what God is going to do, but rejoice in the fact that He already has the situation in His hands. He has done it before, and He will carry you through every time. "My brethren, count it all joy when you fall into various trials, knowing that the testing of you faith produces patience." (James 1:2-4) It goes on to say that "If any of you lacks wisdom, let him ask of God, who gives to all liberally and without reproach, and it will be given to him. But let him ask in faith, with no doubting, for he who doubts is like a wave of the sea driven and tossed by the wind." (James 5-7). God says we only have to ask, He is waiting to hear from us and will give us the Wisdom we need.

Chapter 19

A New Heart

As the years passed by, my mum and I would still think about the very special blessing and privilege when God healed her in the ambulance, and we would go over every detail, in awe of it all. Every time we talked about it, more and more would be revealed. We just loved going over and over it and re-living her Miracle. She never ever had another stroke. Her life changed so much, and she, at last, could be the wonderful person God created her to be. She was full of love, compassion, laughter, joy and loved life, free of all the bitterness, anger and heavy burdens she carried most of her life. No more depression or unforgiveness. It was so lovely to see her enjoying herself and loved so much by her grandchildren and children. Everyone noticed the difference in her. She was also a lot more tolerant with my father. He had to work a lot harder to wind her up.

♥

My mum had started coming to Church with me and my partner, John. It was a lovely Pentecostal Church which held a few hundred people in their services. They did a lot with the local community and schools as well. They also have a Healing Centre every Saturday morning between 10-12 o'clock, where ministers from about 20 different Churches would come together to pray for the sick or for anyone who needed prayer. It's a beautiful time with worship, music, prayer, and just basking in the glorious presence of our Holy Spirit and a time to share Communion. When you arrived at the

Healing Centre, you would collect a number and then wait to be called in for prayer; meanwhile, the beautiful Christian music was playing, and people were praying and worshipping and blessing one another. Wouldn't it be wonderful if all GP surgeries were like that. Then, they would call you to go into the next room for prayer, or sometimes it was held in the actual Church, which had lots of chairs and sofas around to sit on and relax after you had prayer, listening to the music in the presence of our wonderful Lord and Saviour, or just lay on the large cushions on the floor, or even paint or do something creative if you wanted to.

My mum really loved going there, she loved the people, and they loved her. I would never have believed years ago that my mum would have gone to anything like this, let alone absolutely love it. It was her time now. She could totally be herself with God. No one to challenge her or tell her she didn't know what she was talking about or that she wasn't good enough. She knew that Jesus loved her. Look what He had done for her. As they prayed for my mum, they shared with her how much she was loved by God, how He saw all her pain and hurt in her life and that God had never left her side and was with her always. They spoke into her life, and she knew it was God speaking to her. She felt so special. I am so pleased that she found a lovely Church and that she didn't have the same opinion as she had before about the church. She actually got to meet God's wonderful people, who were full of His love and compassion and not only that, they knew her, as God was revealing things about her to them.

Family and friends also noticed the difference in her and that she loved going to this Church. They noticed the beautiful peace mum now had; she had changed so much, all that unforgiveness and bitterness had totally gone, and they, too, could see that she was finally free and able to live the abundant life Jesus wants us all to have. Now where my mother and I were not close before her Miracle, we were now bonded, and everyone could see how close this brought us together.

♥

As time went on, mum was getting older, and her body becoming frailer with age. She was now 89. She had lost a lot of weight, her legs were very thin, and she was finding it hard to walk. She used a frame at home, but she still wanted to go to Church, so John and I would take her in a wheelchair as I didn't want her breaking any bones as it was hard enough getting her in and out of the car. She still wanted to go to Church, though. One day when we were at Church, while two people were praying for my mum, a lady came over and asked if she could pray for my mum's legs. Of course, she said she could. She said that God had been speaking to her about my mum's legs. After that, my mum started walking again, unaided and was back to making tea and cooking her own meals in the kitchen. Nothing is too much for God, and there was me accepting her old age and that it was not unusual that she couldn't walk properly and have other ailments connected to being almost 90, but God had other plans, and He healed her of everything that came her way in old age.

♥

I remember one of the times she went to the hospital when she was in her late 80s; they said she had angina, and had also had a mild heart attack. She started to get what they called a "TIA" now and then. We refused to believe that she would suffer again. God healed her of a massive stroke at 79, and she never had another one, and she is not going to leave this world having one. They wanted to do a minor heart operation on her, but she didn't want it, nor did I want it for her. God has healed her before; He will do it again. She never in her whole life had a major operation (only on her appendix when she was much younger, which turned out it wasn't needed to be done anyway). The doctors had said that she was very frail and it was a risk. She didn't feel happy about having it, and we spoke on our own one night at the hospital. A nurse happened to come along while I was still there; she was not part of the team but just seemed to be passing by, and she said to my mum that she didn't think she should have the operation. It was almost confirmation that God had sent, and that made up her mind. Maybe she was an Angel too? So after that, my mum decided not to have the operation. She also said that one night a man appeared to her in her hospital room; she said that he was standing by the window and said that she was going to be healed at Church.

Some months later, I was speaking to a friend of mine whose mother had the same operation that my mum was asked to have. Her mother wasn't as old as my mum, but sadly she didn't make it, and my friend felt so bad because her mother had told her that she didn't want the operation. God bless them.

When my mum came out of the hospital, we went back to Church, to the Healing Centre, and while we were there, one of the prayer team ministers, who was praying for my mum, said to her, "God told me this morning, that He was going to give someone a New Heart". And God healed my mum again at Church. God gave her a New Heart, as He promised, and she never had another TIA again. She trusted God, and He healed her. And everyone around her saw that she had no more TIA's and was much healthier again.

Chapter 20

Christmas Dinner

I am so glad that my son invited my mum and dad for Christmas dinner at our house in Christmas 2015. It gave her yet more things to plan out, even though she was almost 90. She loved a list, and we all had our orders, amongst which were; strictly no crackers or hats. My son would be cooking the turkey, as she didn't trust me to cook it. I think that was because the last time I cooked Christmas dinner for them, I left the bag of giblets in the turkey, and she said I could have poisoned them all. My sister had orders what she had to bring, and my mum didn't want me to do the vegetables because she said 'they were too hard.' She would do the Brussels sprouts and some other bits herself. I could get the deserts, and a box of custard, which I would buy ready-made from the shop, so I really didn't have to do much.

What she didn't know was that my son had so much to drink the night before; on Christmas Eve, he had a hangover and was in bed most of the morning, so I had to cook the turkey. My mum said it was delicious, thinking that my son had cooked it, and of course, he enjoyed getting the praise for it, saying "Thanks, nannie." at the same time looking at me with a big smile. She never knew any different. And as for the 'no hats and crackers', I have plenty of photos of her asleep on my sofa, with her Christmas hat on.

♥

We decided to have a big party for my mum's 90th birthday, which was in April 2016. We hired a nice hall, and she did a lot of the organising herself, of course, and chose all the music, most of which was from the 40s,50s,60s and 70s. She was getting more and more frail but was still very "with it", as she liked to say. She wanted everything planned out, to every detail, and the family all mucked in. Her party was brilliant, it went just as she had planned, even better, and she had about 70 people there. She also gave a lovely speech about her family and her faith in God.

♥

Around the same time, she arranged lunch at a restaurant, where just her five children and spouses joined her and my dad. John and I were running late, but when we approached the table, to our surprise, everyone's heads were bowed, they were all holding hands, and my mum was praying for her family and thanking God. I was a bit disappointed that we missed my mum's prayers, as this is something so new for all the family to see, but thinking about it all, I believe I was meant to miss it because if I had been there, everyone would have thought that I had put my mum up to it, not that I could have done if she didn't want to of course, but this way, they could see it came naturally from her heart. She totally took control as head of the family, and she thanked God. I was in awe to see how God had changed her life and how natural prayer was to her now. It wasn't my father praying, who always did, but even he knew that my mum was at one with God.

When she realised that I wasn't there from the beginning, she was very disappointed too; she said that she thought we were at the other end of the table. I assured her that it was meant to be; everyone could see how important God is to her and knew it was something she wanted to do herself.

♥

The next thing on her list was, planning her funeral. Now please don't stop reading this and think that I am being morbid, although many years ago, I would probably have put the book down. I have been working at a lovely local Law Firm for the past 15 years in the Private Client department, which deals with Wills, Lasting Powers of Attorney and also Probates. Since working there, I have come to realise the importance of getting things in order; if they aren't, it can be even more stressful for those left behind. So to be able to talk about it all, I realised, was part of life and very important.

My mum wanted us to drive her around the cemeteries. There was a new cemetery opened locally, and when we went there, it was like heavenly gardens on earth. I knew she was preparing herself, just by all the things she said and did, and it was getting clearer that she had had enough of life here in her frail little body. Her mind was still very active, and she was still gently feisty if she wanted to be, but she was filled with such peace, acceptance, love and harmony, she had no doubt about where she was going, and Heaven was waiting for her. She pointed to a nice plot to be buried at the cemetery and wanted a white stone with grey writing. Yet another list was created of things to do, every detail, the music, the hymns, the prayers, but I had to stop her when she started talking about the part when they put the mud on her. Too much information.

Chapter 21

You are Forgiven

It was early September 2016, and my mum was in the bathroom when she accidentally bumped her shin. As she hardly had any flesh on her legs, and her skin was very thin, she, unfortunately, ended up with a big blister on her leg. The nurse from the GP Surgery came to the house and dressed it, but days went by, and it wasn't healing very well. Eventually, she was taken to hospital, as the blister, which was now the size of a ring doughnut, had travelled around her shin to the back of her leg and looked like it was going to burst. They kept her in the hospital. She was heavily medicated because of the pain, and a couple of times, they were quite worried about her. Because of the medication they put her on, she was asleep most of the time we visited, and the bandage around her leg was very thick.

Eventually, she came around a bit, and we were able to speak to her when we visited, but she was still very heavily sedated. She seemed to be going through the mill there, and we couldn't understand why, as it was only a blister that she went in with.

One day when I visited her, she said to me that she had a dream, that there were different boxes and one had a frog in it. She said there were Angels with beautiful flowers all over their gowns. And then she saw Jesus, with His arms open wide to her, and He said to her, "You are forgiven". Even though she was still very tired, she managed to explain this all to me. She also told other members of the family about it.

I talked about her coming home, and she said to me in a very positive, rational manner, "I'm not coming home, Derrice". "You are mum". I told her, but underneath I knew that my mum knew that she would soon be leaving this world; she knew she wasn't going to be leaving the hospital. She was preparing for her heavenly home, and in a funny sort of way, she was preparing me, too, for her leaving this world. She was always so kind to other patients when she was in the hospital; I remember once she said the lady in the next bed wanted a cuddle, so she got out of bed and gave her one, but this time, she couldn't do that as she was unable to get out of bed by herself.

We kept mum as comfortable as possible. Some days she would respond and was up talking quite awake and chatty. Other days she was sleeping. She was still very "with it," as she told one of the doctors one day when he commented to her that she was very "with it." She told us what he had said and that she replied, "Yes, I'm "with it!" using her two fingers in the air as speech marks.

I remember going one night to visit her, and I found one of her tablets on the floor; it was quite a large tablet. I picked it up as she lay there and said to her, very concerned, "Mum, is this one of your tablets? It was on the floor!" She lay there quite chilled out until I said that, and suddenly she waved her arm frantically, shouting at me, "Shut up! It's too big. I'm not having it". She knew it was there; she had thrown it on the floor herself. It did make me laugh. She was so funny, without even realising it.

Things were not all that great for her sometimes in the hospital at the end; I hate to say it. She said one night, she was very shaky and was calling out for help. She said a nurse came and stood at the curtain by her bed. My mum asked her if she could hold her hand, but she didn't; she just stood there looking at my mum without a care in the world for her. My mum was quite upset about that when she told us about it. She must have been so desperate to do that, as she was quite a strong person, and maybe as her family weren't there, she looked at a nurse to show her some compassion, but she didn't. When I thought about that, I felt quite upset, but God said to me, "Don't worry; you should know I was holding her hand." And He was. As He always did. I knew that from her Angel encounter, her Angel was there with her again.

One evening, it was a couple of days before she was due to come home from the hospital, we went to visit her, and they told us she would be home by the weekend. We were so pleased. My mum was really on the ball and back to her feisty self in the nicest possible way. I fed her with her favourite jelly and raspberries. She lapped it up and then told me off for feeding her too fast, "Stop stuffing it in!" She said. We were laughing. The hospital told us that she should be going home at the weekend. I was excited to hear that. She seemed so much better.

The following evening we went to see her, but when we arrived, there was a lot of fuss going on around her bed, the curtains were drawn, and nurses and doctors were running around. I asked if everything was ok, and they said yes, they will speak to us in a minute; and they asked us to wait outside. As the commotion was going on, I noticed there was an opening in one of the curtains, and I peered through and saw a lot of blood on a rolled-up bed sheet, which was on the chair. I was very concerned and asked what was happening, and they said that the doctor would speak to us soon. We waited, wondering what was going on, as she was so good when we left her the night before.

Eventually, the doctor came out to see us and told us that my mum isn't well. I asked what was wrong, but she didn't really give a full answer. She just said she is not very well at all. On reflection, I should have pursued it more, but I was in a bit of shock as she was so good yesterday I couldn't take in what she was telling us, feeling like I was in a bubble again. You rely on the doctors, but what happened doesn't seem to make sense. The doctor told us that mum is not good at all; she didn't know how long she had left. She said I should speak to the rest of the family. I said she was ok yesterday. I asked what was going on, and she said her bowl was twisted. I suddenly thought I hoped it wasn't the Jelly, but they assured me it wasn't that. They said to call in the morning and speak to a doctor again. No one else from the family was there at the time, only John and myself. I didn't challenge it because, as I said, you rely on the doctors, but this really didn't add up. We couldn't go back in to see my mum as there was a lot going on, and the doctor ushered us out.

I went home and called my siblings to let them know what the doctor had said, and they too were quite shocked, as they thought my mum was coming home at the weekend. They had also seen her the day before, and she was very good, sitting up in bed. I know it has been said that sometimes people seem better before they go, but what was all the blood on the sheets about.

The next day, we were getting ready to head to the hospital in the morning. One of my sisters called me. She was at the hospital already; she had called the hospital in the morning, and they told her that my mum was not good and that we should all get to the hospital. I should have asked what all the blood was.

Chapter 22

Angels

10 October 2016

11.00 am

It was a beautiful sunny day. When I got to the hospital, the curtains were drawn around my mum's bed in the ward. My three sisters were by her bedside, and my dad was holding onto my mum's hand, stroking her hair, which she always loved him doing. He looked so sad. She was quite still and peaceful, and her mouth was open, but you could see that life was slowly drifting out of her. She held on for us. I called my brother, and he was already on his way. She looked so beautiful, like sleeping beauty. My dad was kissing her and telling her how much he loves her. We had all been kissing her and spending time with her in our own ways, even leading up to this day, on our individual visits to the hospital. It was very special.

We felt we should leave my mum and dad alone together for a while, and we went along to the day room along the corridor. The Doctor came and had a chat with us and said that mum's kidneys had stopped working. He said we could be there a while, but it was difficult to say. One of my siblings suggested that we go and get some coffee and something to eat from the hospital café. I was concerned, as I felt I didn't want to leave then, in case anything happened, and none of us would be there with her; although my dad was there, I wanted us all to be with her when she finally left. I had a strong urge to go back to my mum before going to the café, so I went back to see her, and I kissed her cheeks while laying my head on her pillow next to her, stroking her beautiful face and letting her know we are all near, hugging her and cuddling her, and telling her that God loves her so much, she knows that, He sent his Angel last time for her and her Angel will be with her again. God has blessed her so much. I said to her that her mum and dad were looking over her, and her brother, our uncle Billy, aunty Yvonne, her best friend Biddy, and most of all, that Jesus loves her and is with her holding her in His hands, and not to worry about anything. She will be ok; Heaven is waiting for her. It was just how I thought it would be, by her bed at the time. While I was speaking to her, she seemed like she was trying to move her head slightly, as though she was trying to say something to me. I now realise that she was probably trying to say goodbye, for now, and yes, that Jesus is there with her, with His Angles. I left her with my dad but still felt very apprehensive about leaving, thinking at the back of my mind that for the sake of having a coffee, we may miss one of the most important times of our lives. But the Doctor had said it might be a while, and I didn't want to leave the others waiting for me. We then went down to the hospital café to get some drinks and sandwiches. We had literally just ordered our food and sat down at the table to eat it when the Doctor phoned one of my sisters on her mobile and said to come up; it was an emergency. We left all our food on the table and rushed up to my mum's ward. We were told to go into the day room. The Doctor came in with his head down and said sorry, but my mum had gone. At least my dad was with her. We went in quietly to my mum's bedside, and my poor dad was crying out for my mum. We had to go and console him. He said she went so peacefully. No shortness of breath or anything. She looked so beautiful, as though she was sleeping and would wake up. While we were all round her bed, I felt the most powerful presence of God that whooshed over us all. I knew God was there. It was a privilege yet again to be by her bedside and feel the powerful presence of God, just like in the ambulance. I then felt led for all of us to hold hands with each other, and my mum, in a prayer chain and pray. We thanked God for her and committed her spirit to Jesus, and we all said prayers. After that, the presence of God was soooooo strong in the room, near the head of her bed, on the right-hand side of her. It took my breath away, and I knew it was Jesus and His Angels waiting for us all to say our bye-byes, and then He would take her with them to Heaven. I asked one of my sisters to come and stand near the head of the bed, and she felt the powerful presence of God, too; she was way swaying and said it was like waves of God's power and presence; we could hardly stand up. We didn't want to leave my dear mummy. I kept kissing her, as we all did because she looked like she would wake up any minute. Her hands felt so soft and her skin beautiful, but experiencing the very presence of God gave us such peace; I cannot tell you how much. We are so grateful. God is amazing. It was the same feeling as in the ambulance, but this time, it was for all of us as well. We were given as long as it took us to let her go, and His presence was there waiting. I know it 100 per cent.

Chapter 23

The White Feather

My mum had to deal with one thing after another but overcame them all. At 90, her mind was still very "with it," as she says, but her body was wearing out; it was tiring just looking at her. We can pray and pray, and God is gracious and answers our prayers, but there is a time we have to let go for their sakes. It is selfish of us to want to keep her. She had a knack for knowing. She knew she wouldn't be coming out of the hospital. She had another encounter with Jesus in the hospital when He appeared to her with His arms open wide. She said there were Angels with flowers all over their garments. I had a dream of a similar thing around the same time; only the Angels in my dream had coloured lights all over their garments.

God gave us time. 10 years ago, she had a stroke, and God healed her in the ambulance. He could have taken her then. She had a miraculous recovery. She even gave her Testimony on Revelation TV, the lovely Christian Chanel I have already mentioned, which is full of inspiration and anything and everything you would want to know to help you in your daily lives. She would never have done anything like that before, and she felt privileged to share it with the world. It totally changed her life and inspired many others, and she had no fear of death; she knew only too well that she wouldn't be alone and that God was with her.

God healed her heart, her TIA's, and so much more. Whatever was thrown at her, God pulled her through it. His Grace is truly "Amazing Grace." She didn't leave this world due to any of the challenges she had suffered. The only operation she had in her life was having her appendix out, and like I have already said, even that turned out to be unnecessary.

Again, God gave us time, 6 weeks while she was in the hospital. Dad was on his own at home having to deal with it, so it wasn't such as much of a shock that she was not in her bed at home, although we so much want her with us forever.

God worked it out that only dad was with her at the time of her death. The two of them. Who, although they had their troubles in life, loved each other so dearly and couldn't live without each other. It all worked out.

♥

Needless to say, her funeral went as planned, as she planned, and even better. Everyone said how beautiful it was, and kept referring to it as "Wedding" but apologised afterwards. I said, please don't apologise; if that is how good it was, then that is what we wanted to hear. One of my sisters had chosen a song to play while the photos were being shown on the screen at the Church. It was the theme to Forest Gump, at the end when the feather is flying around. It went really well with the photo slide show that was being shown at her funeral. She had beautiful hymns and prayers, and her grandchildren spoke about her, my brother also did, and John sang 'Amazing Grace' for her. It was all so very special, and God was the centre of it all.

Everyone was standing around her as they lowered her, and we had the beautiful song 'Alleluia' playing as people were given a basket of rose petals to throw in and, yes, a basket of mud. She knew everything. We had two white doves, which flew off from by the side where they laid her to rest. Later that day, one of my sisters said to me, "Did you see the white feather on the floor?" I hadn't seen it, and if I had, I would have picked it up. I wish I had seen it.

The next day my son and I went to the 'garden', as I like to call it, to see all the flowers where my mother lay. As we were standing there by her plot, I looked down, and there was the beautiful white feather; it must have fallen from one of the doves. This must be the one my sister was talking about. I couldn't believe it was still there, so I picked it up. I have it in a lovely white frame with a blue sky background.

Chapter 24

Feathers Everywhere

Do you know, I see feathers everywhere. There are certain types of feathers. Sometimes they just float down out of nowhere in front of me when I am walking along. They have even appeared at my office desk on two occasions. I found one on the floor at the bank, in a coffee shop, and in the most unusual places. And sometimes, when I am upset about my mum, a feather appears out of nowhere.

Not only are they actual feathers that appear, but the shapes of the clouds are sometimes actual feathers. I will speak about this later. That is why I talk about the feathers in the sky, the feather clouds.

My son and my nephew have both had very vivid dreams of my mum. They said in the dreams; she was talking to them as though she was there. She said to them to talk to her like they always did. She said she can see us, but we can't see her.

I also had two dreams about her, where she looked younger and was smiling and very happy.

I feel how important it was now that my sister chose the feather song for the music, as feathers really mean something to us now, and I have seen them ever since. Maybe it's God's way of allowing His Angels to show us that she is ok. We could feel my mum around us. She is the most wonderful mother and grandmother. Her grandchildren love her so much. She is so unselfish, always giving everything for her family and others and keeping nothing for herself.

We love her so much, and so do many others whose lives she has touched. She has left a legacy. Thank you, God. She is now in Heaven with Jesus and her parents and relatives, and friends. We will all meet one day again. God bless our dear mum, and thank you, God, for your Amazing Grace and Love.

♥

It seemed like my mum was flying around with the Angels, there is even a song called 'Flying with Angels', which we played and played, and that describes it all. Like she was free, enjoying her freedom, and full of happiness, love and laughter. Flying with her friends and Angels. It felt like she had asked Jesus if she could just be around to see us for a while. What we were experiencing was love. All around us. Angels leaving feathers to let us know that she is ok and happy. There were so many feathers, too much to be a coincidence. Here are just some of them.

I was sitting in a café in London not long after she passed. We had gone to the Shard with some friends, but I didn't want to go up to the top, as I don't like heights, so I decided to go into a café and have a coffee while they went up to look at it. I was right at the back of this café, enjoying a mocha and obviously thinking about my lovely mum. There on the floor, right by my shoe, was a pure white feather. I picked it up and kept it. I know anyone can say that a feather can turn up or blow in or be stuck to your shoe, but the feathers I saw seemed to be special types of feathers like you knew they were different, they were left by an Angel for comfort and it was a message with it, knowing it was to do with my mum. Pure white. People who were with me began to realise this, too and witnessed the feathers. They were in the most unusual places, and always when I was deep in thought about my mum or talking about her. I have collected so many of them.

One day I went to my car, and literally where the windscreen wiper was stood a beautiful large white feather, placed there. There is no way that it could have landed the way it did, as it was definitely placed there. I believe by an Angel.

I have found on two separate occasions feathers in my office. How do they get into the office. White ones. They are special feathers, not like normal ones. Pretty fluffy or curved with fluffy at the end.

When my sister and I were on holiday in Portugal, we were walking along talking about our mum, and suddenly, a pure white feather gracefully floated down in front of us.

Also, the very Christmas of 2016, the lights in London were feathers and Angels.

After my mum's experience with Angels, and the Bible is full of Angels, I believe they are here for us, looking after us. Psalm 91 says that God gives his Angels charge over us to protect us and be with us wherever we go. I have always believed in Angels, but I now realise and understand their purpose so much more. They are not just Christmas decorations; they are very real, sent from Heaven for you and me.

Chapter 25

My lovely Dad

My dear dad never got over my mum's passing. He was very sad and was never quite himself again. He missed her so much. He said she would be talking to him some nights, sitting in her chair, which was still there. He kept everything that belonged to her in its place. All her clothes were hanging in her wardrobe, nothing was touched in her room, and everything was left as if she was still there. He got more and more dependent upon his family, and from the night my mum passed away, my siblings and I took turns to stay over night with him. We didn't want to leave him on his own as he was getting very frail himself. He said that he didn't want to go into a care home, and I wouldn't have done anything against his wishes. They looked after us when we were young, and now it was our turn to look after them when they needed us.

As time went on, he needed more help, and we had to get some carers in to look after him as well. This is not how he wanted to live, and his quality of life got worse, and he ended up not being able to walk unassisted. He had a hoist, his bed, and everything he needed in his large front room, which he now lived in.

I had many lovely conversations with my dad too, and he really missed my mum. My poor dad was getting frailer and was now 94. I asked God if He could make a way that I could be with my dad the night before he went to Heaven. God never fails, and it is amazing how He works things out. I didn't want my dad alone at any time, even though he had 24-hour care in the end with a lovely care agency, the girls were like angels, and he loved them all, and they loved him. But even though he had a lovely live-in carer, she needed her sleep, and I wanted to make sure that my dad was not alone at night in his room and that someone was with him, so I arranged for an overnight carer to sit with him while he slept. One particular weekend I couldn't get an overnight carer. I tried, but no one was available. John and I decided to stay with my dad, and we both slept overnight on the sofa bed, as we did before the 24-hour live-in carer came to stay. This particular night I slept in the chair holding my dad's hand all night to let him know that I was with him and keep him comforted. We stayed on the Saturday night, but the Sunday night, I stayed alone with my dad. He seemed a bit unsettled and was in and out of consciousness, as he had been for the last couple of days. I kept getting up to see to him and let him know that I was there.

In the morning, he was not very with it, so I called the Marie Curie nurses, who I had previously spoken to, and a wonderful nurse came straight away. Sadly, she said it wouldn't be long. I had already called my siblings and family to let them know. It was the most beautiful sunny day, and the sky was like I had never seen it before. The family arrived, and we each spent time with my dad during the day. When I went outside into the garden and looked up at the sky, above the bungalow was the biggest, most beautiful white feather cloud hovering over the house. It was there for hours. **The feather cloud on the front cover of this book is the actual cloud that I am talking about**. I was thinking, what a lovely sunny day it was for him to go to Heaven on the clouds. A feather cloud, my mum, must have been waiting.

Here is the photo of the cloud:

I put a large photo of my mum beside him on his bed and his Bible under his hand as he lay there sleeping, physically unresponsive to what was going on around him, but I am sure he could see everything clearly. My sister had put on his favourite music, which played continuously all day. It eventually got to the evening, and my son and his girlfriend were on their way. Everyone else was there, including my nephew and his girlfriend, but my son had to work, and he was working quite a distance away, so he couldn't get back until late. They arrived eventually at 11.00 p.m., and we were all there around my dad's bed. He waited for them; he didn't want to go before they arrived. He had his family around him, just as he wanted. By 11.25, I felt led to say the Lord's Prayer, and we all held hands around his bed, and after we had prayed, I watched as his body gently moved, and he took a sigh, and I knew that his spirit had just left him. How beautifully graceful. I can't believe that I would ever say that because no one wants to see that happen, but it was his time, and he wanted to go, and he had no quality of life left in him; he said that he didn't want to be here anymore. It wasn't morbid as I thought it would be, maybe because I had already seen my mum after she had passed away, but to actually witness his spirit leave his body, was somewhat incredible. He was now at peace. We all stayed by him for a couple of hours until he was collected from the house. Almost three years after my mum had passed away, my dad was finally with her again, rejoicing in Heaven.

The very next day, the lovely live-in carer who had been looking after my dad, and knew that I was feather mad, called me up. She said that she was hoovering, and suddenly a white feather flew in from outside into the kitchen where she was, and it landed on her jumper. She took a photo of it and sent it to me. "Now I believe what you are talking about ". She said.

Chapter 26

Clouds in the sky

I love all the seasons, but summer is my favourite. It was a lovely sunny July afternoon, a little too hot to sit out in the sunshine for too long, so I went inside to cool off for a while. I put on a light-hearted uplifting film and sat on my cool leather sofa with my cup of tea and a plate of shortbread biscuits, feet up, relaxing and enjoying the film. A bright ray of glistening sunshine suddenly beamed through the tilted white Venetian blinds on the front window, lighting up the whole room. I went over to the window and opened the shutter, and I was greeted by a golden ball of sunlight reflecting off the window of the house on the opposite side of the road. I just love it. I peered through, looking up at the beautiful deep blue sky, and yes, there it was a pure white perfectly formed feather cloud. I immediately reached for my phone, ready to take yet more photos of clouds, and headed for the back garden again to get a full view.

Looking up, I smiled, not just one feather cloud anymore, but two, always two now, one for my mum and one for my dad. I clicked away, taking lots of photos from all different angles wanting to capture everything I could, well aware of the amount of photos I was taking, but thinking at the same time that I would sort through them later and delete the repeats, which I never actually did, the memory in my phone was getting fuller by the minute, but I couldn't lose any of the photos, they were far too precious.

I sat down in the garden on my comfortable lounger under the sun umbrella for a while, watching the feather-shaped clouds and soaking up the energy from them as they stood still, hovering over me. They didn't seem to move or change shape for a long time, unlike the puffy white clouds which drifted slowly by. The sky was so blue, and the pure white clouds stood out as though they had been placed there, like a painting. I was sitting there thinking about my dad, feeling that I didn't see all the feathers everywhere that I did when my mum passed away, and that was ok, but just thinking about him and wondering what he was doing in Heaven. I was looking for a sign. I looked up at the sky again, and there was a cloud in the shape of an elephant. The elephant meant a lot to me, as I have mentioned in this book, relating to my dad, who told us stories about them.

This is another elephant cloud I saw on another occasion. Again, by the time I took the photo, it had moved slightly. And instead of seeing feathers everywhere, which I saw with my mum, everything with my dad seems to relate to elephants, and not only clouds.

These are very special clouds; I really feel that they are Heaven-sent and that God's Angels play a bit part in placing them there for us at particular times to bring comfort and assurance to us, as they always do and from time to time they bring a tangible presence with them like God himself is speaking to us.

I have always found clouds fascinating. One of the first things I do when I wake up in the morning is to look at them, and as the day goes by, I keep looking up at the sky. Yes, the clouds can tell us what sort of day it's going to be; if they are grey and cloudy, it's probably going to rain or thunder, but I don't mean it that way. When you study them, they seem to have a pattern to them.

We used to drive to Spain on holiday every year and did so for about 12 years. I would love looking up at the clouds; you can see so much in them. I have seen giant Angels in the shapes of clouds, I saw the hand of God, and many other shapes, which I have drawn and made a note of the date and time I saw them.

I had the most beautiful dream one night, or vision; I am not sure, it was so realistic, as though I was actually there, and I remember it as clearly today as I did then. It was in the year 2000. It was Jesus high up in the clouds standing on a beautiful white pillar, which seemed to be very long and never-ending, as I couldn't see the bottom of it as it went way down and disappeared into the puffy white clouds below. Jesus' arms were open wide, and a beautiful white Dove was hovering behind him. The dream was just a beautiful blue sky and pure white clouds. No other colours in it apart from blue and white. I tried to draw the vision, but I am not artistic in any way. This was many years ago, but years later, I was looking on the internet, and I was so amazed to see a picture of Jesus in the clouds with his arms open, on a pillar, with a white Dove behind him. I know people may think that I could have seen the picture and dreamt about it, but it wasn't like a dream; it was so real. I remember feeling afterwards that I had been in the very presence of Jesus and that he allowed me to see this, and for days and weeks, and now years later, it feels like it was only yesterday, and still so clear and vivid, and I was pleased to see a similar picture, which describes it better than I could have drawn it.

I really believe that clouds are very relevant. I started writing down the dates and times, and as I said, I would try to draw images of what I saw. Eventually, I started to keep a camera handy, so I could take photos of them, which I have been doing since, although now I use my mobile phone and not a camera. There seems to be a pattern to clouds. I noticed that some days there would be animal faces in the clouds, bears hugging or close to each other, dogs, dolphins, and humans too. I know it sounds mad, but if you try it, you will see exactly what I mean. There is even a cloud society on the internet where people connect clouds to God. Actually, while writing this book, I looked up clouds in the Bible and found so much information and how they are related to God, which I set out below.

"Then I looked, and behold, a white cloud, and seated on the cloud one like a son of man, with a golden crown on his head, and a sharp sickle in his hand." (Revelation 14:14)

"Then we who are alive, who are left, will be caught up together with them in the clouds to meet the Lord in the air, and so we will always be with the Lord." (1 Thessalonians 4:17)

Then I saw another mighty angel coming down from heaven, wrapped in a cloud, with a rainbow over his head, and his face was like the sun, and his legs like pillars of fire." (Revelation 10:1)

"And as soon as Aaron spoke to the whole congregation of the people of Israel, they looked toward the wilderness, and behold, the glory of the Lord appeared in the cloud." (Exodus 16:10).

In the Bible, God used a cloud for Moses to lead His people. "And the Lord went before them by day in a pillar of cloud to lead them along the way, and by night in a pillar of fire to give them light, that they might travel by day and by night. " (Revelation 11:12).

"For your steadfast love is great above the heavens; your faithfulness reaches to the clouds." (Exodus 24:16)

And Jesus said, "I am, and you will see the Son of Man seated at the right hand of Power, and coming with the clouds of heaven." (Mark 14:62)

"He lays the beams of his chambers on the waters; he makes the clouds his chariot; he rides on the wings of the wind; " (Psalm 104:3)

And the Lord said to Moses, "Behold, I am coming to you in a thick cloud, that the people may hear when I speak with you, and may also believe you forever." (Exodus 19:9)

And then they will see the Son of Man coming in clouds with great power and glory. (Mark 13:26)

"Behold, he is coming with the clouds, and every eye will see him, even those who pierced him, and all tribes of the earth will wail on account of him. Even so. Amen." (Revelation 1:7)

He was still speaking when, behold, a bright cloud overshadowed them, and a voice from the cloud said, "This is my beloved Son, with whom I am well pleased; listen to him." (Matthew 17:5)

"And when he had said these things, as they were looking on, he was lifted up, and a cloud took him out of their sight." (Acts 1:9)

And at the seventh time he said, "Behold, a little cloud like a man's hand is rising from the sea." And he said, "Go up, say to Ahab, 'Prepare your chariot and go down, lest the rain stop you.'" And in a little while the heavens grew black with clouds and wind, and there was a great rain. And Ahab rode and went to Jezreel." (1 Kings 18:44-45)

"I do set my bow in the cloud, and it shall be a token of a covenant between me and the earth" (Genesis 9:13)

Chapter 27

Reminiscing

It was a blustery Sunday afternoon. I pulled up outside the bungalow to see the 'FOR SALE' sign sitting amongst the overgrown conifers, which brought me to tears. The familiar look of the sweet bungalow. Nothing changes; it looks the same as it always has done for the past 40 years.

Approaching the bungalow, putting the key in the front door again had that homely feeling drawing me to it, only this time, it was to the sounds of silence. No loud TV blaring or the smell of cooking coming from the kitchen, no overhearing voices from family members who had come to visit at the weekend, as they often did, but just the fading smell of what was, still lingered. With a slight dampness adding to the aroma. I couldn't hold the tears from flowing as I looked into the emptiness of the bungalow. I looked to the right where my mum's bedroom was, but just the pink curtains left hanging, no furniture, just bare walls and carpet, with marks where her chair and bed had once been. The last memories of her in her bedroom were when she was very frail; she was 90, so she had reason to be. It was lovely tucking her up in bed with her little lamp on and her soft, pretty light duvet. I wish she could have stayed at home and not gone to the hospital.

Looking to the left was my dad's bedroom, not as cute, but more rugged looking, a mantle piece on which he kept my mum's lipstick and perfume on after she passed away. The brown curtains that hid the sunshine from coming in the morning so he could lay in, as he had been up all night watching TV. When they were up and about, my mum usually fell asleep earlier but would get up in the night for a midnight feast; then, my dad would wake up and join her.

Looking at the torn wallpaper next to where my dad's duvet lay. It bothered him so much, but no one seemed to have the time to help fix it. He would have done it in his younger days. It frustrated him to know that he couldn't do it anymore.

As I passed through the hallway to check that my tears hadn't smudged my mascara, I realised the mirror was no longer in there; it had long gone to the charity shop along with all the furniture and everything else. How empty it looked without all their bits and pieces on the walls. A plaque showing The Lord's Prayer was on the wall in the hallway. It was quite a large spacious bungalow, but when my mum and dad lived in it, it was full of family clutter, unwanted gifts from people, along with so many family photos; you could hardly see the walls. Every surface was cluttered with photos. My mum and dad must have felt obliged to put them up, although they loved their family. My mum's paper cuttings were stuffed into her bedroom chest of drawers, from Christmas and birthday cards, paper bags, the cellophane from cards, she kept it all.

The bathroom was empty, with only a hand wash and a small towel left. All the memories in there from their latter years, from sponging my mum down, washing her hair, also to get my dad to the toilet on his Zimmer frame. The smell of Dettol and old spice. Along with other smells that came later.

The empty kitchen which was the heart of the house. My mum and dad were always in there cooking, making tea, eating; the family was in and out when they visited, helping themselves to cakes and biscuits. The fridge was always full of sweet things. Tea mugs with 'Best Granddad' and 'Best Nanny'. My mum's special cooking pan and my dad's very old rusty spatulas. Now there are empty spaces where the washing machine and freezer once stood. An empty cupboard, which once housed the best glasses, that only came out when we had guests. Looking at the little cooker there, remembering my mum's special pan that she had had for years, it was totally burnt. She would spend hours soaking her pots and pans, and the sound of her scouring them made my skin shiver. They had nice new pans, but they said they were too good to use, just like many other presents, which included a Teasmaid that I bought them for their 25th Wedding Anniversary, which was kept in the loft, still in its box, never used.

And finally, the living room. The red carpet looked so worn and threadbare in some places now. The broken Venetians were never fixed. The bare walls where all the photos once were now just show the nails that held them there. You could count the photos just by the outline of the shapes on the walls, where the original paper hadn't faded behind the photos. Cellotape where the old Christmas decorations were stuck to the walls. All the lovely memories of the family gatherings, birthdays, Christmas dinners, and music playing loudly. My mum and dad loved watching lovely old afternoon films. Laughter of the family gatherings echoed from the walls, the grandchildren running around, birthday cakes and anniversary occasions, opening presents.

The only things left on top of the fireplace surround were two Christmas cards addressed to my mum and dad. One was from my son, and the other was from my nephew, each with their own lovely words and saying to Nannie and Granddad to have a happy

Christmas in Heaven. The other two cards were the ones that my mum and dad gave each other on their 70th Wedding Anniversary.

Looking through the large picture windows at the rear of the lounge into the now-overgrown garden. It would never have looked like this. My dad would be out there every day with his cap on, wearing pink sunglasses that he bought from the charity shop, mowing the lawn or cutting back the bushes, shaping them, and the garden was perfect. My mum used to love her garden but had given up on it. She would just watch him work from her chair while watching TV at the same time, giving orders. The old bird cage, which once had a flowerpot in it, is still in the tree, although the flowers are long gone. The garden gnomes and ornaments lying around looked old and tattered, as they hadn't been painted for years. Looking at the greenhouse that my mum so wanted, but what ended up as storage for everything but plants. The shed, with the broken window from the football that the boys kicked into it, was never fixed.

The music player that my dad listened to was still in the bungalow, sitting on a table with a lamp that had a timer on it. The family kept it there to play when anyone of us visited to check the house for mail. That was all that was left of the memories. It will stay there until contracts were exchanged; then, that will be the last thing to go. The music is all my mum and dad's music. So lovely to listen to it. Bringing back memories of my mum singing along to Doris Day and my dad singing louder and louder just to annoy her.

My mum's beautiful red rose bush, just outside the back window. I remember when she passed away, it had never been in such full bloom. Beautiful bright red roses. She loved her roses.

New families will move in and make their own beautiful memories like we all once did when the people who lived there before us moved out.

The loft is now clear. They were too old to get up there. My dad always kept it clean, hoovered, and sprayed. He used to ask me what it looked like since he was not able to get up there. I said I had cleaned it, but it was nothing like he used to do. He would be pleased when I told him I had wiped off the cobwebs.

Looking up at the ceiling fan. I remember my dad saying, "put the fan on, put the fan on." He loved the fan on all night; he felt so hot at night. I put the fan on again; it spun around and brought back so many memories. Later memories were paramedics attending or carers coming in and out, nurses giving meds, or taking blood, but that didn't override all the wonderful times that we had there before.

I wondered what they are doing in Heaven. How funny life is, all those years you spend knowing what they are doing and where they are, and then one day, they are gone, and you know nothing about them anymore. But if we could see what they were doing, we would not be curious anymore. Having faith in God makes me not worry because I know where they are, and the Bible says what Heaven is like and what Jesus has prepared for those who love him.

The last Christmas my dad was sad because my mum wasn't there anymore. We tried to make the best of it, but it was never the same for him. He missed her so much; he wanted to go to be with her. She really was a rock for him and the family.

Connie Francis comes on, and it takes me back again to mums lovely voice singing along to it when we were younger, while she was cooking. She had a lovely voice. She was so attractive and well dressed, lovely and slim, and my dad always kept himself well, did his exercises every day, and never had weight or a tummy.

How fit they were in their younger days, right up until their 80s, I never knew how they had so much energy. It wasn't until their late 80s that it began to tell, walking slower, hunching over, and generally getting older. Doddering about, so sweetly, like two wind-up toys.

Going into dads little office and his prayer room, where he also kept a chest of drawers and had a little wardrobe with his shirts and trousers and suits for Church. I remember his many ties, cosy cardigans and soft slippers in the room. The chest of drawers held other things, like hair brushes, aftershave, tape measures, batteries, and all the things that daddies kept for jobs to do. Oh, and a toolbox for inside the house. There was the garage, of course, where he kept all his other tools, old mustard or jam jars full of nails, bits of wood, lawnmower, strimmer, you name it.

There were a pile of leaflets and unwanted post building up on the floor. No need to worry about that anymore.

Thank you for the memories, mum and dad.

Leaving the bungalow and seeing the sign outside. Looking back at the night light left on, glowing through the front door window. The bungalow is the same as it has always been, now it is waiting to welcome the next family to make beautiful, happy times in.

Chapter 28

Little notes mean so much

My parents are always with us. Little things we find. I found a lovely note from my mother, it was when I was going through one of my challenging times in the past, and she wrote this little note on one of the tags that she had made from a card, attached to something she had bought me, but I cant remember what it was, but the note said that they are always here for me. That refers to now as well.

Looking back at the birthday cards that she wrote to me, all sorts of things make me laugh now. She really did care and was such a good mother. I am glad I kept lots of my birthday cards from my parents. My mum would always write a lecture about how it's time I grew up and so on, but it was always written with a smile on her face. She was always so thoughtful in her cards and gifts.

Her final wish was granted, that I find a good man, and she loves him. She said she would have to wait to get to Heaven to find her celestial man. But dad is with her now.

When we were growing up, my mum always seemed quite harsh, but she was so full of wisdom. She was very well-read on politics and would have made a great leader. She was a very strong-minded woman, but she would give you the coat off her back if you needed it.

She always said to me to keep a nest egg for myself. Give me £5 a week" she would say so that she could save it for me. This was some years ago. I never did. I now see exactly what she means, and I wished that I had given it to her to save for me. It must have been hard for her to rely on my dad for things, not that she was one to do that. She was very independent, even making money by sewing for others or at boot sales; when we looked at notes on what she made at the boot sales selling her lovely toilet rolls holders, aprons, and things she would make. Stamps. There was hardly anything, £2 here and there. She saved it all up and kept it separate in her own account, away from my dad. Always said to keep a nest egg. Save money. Before she passed, another thing she did, again as a matter of some urgency, as she wanted to distribute her savings to the grandchildren. She didn't want my dad getting his hands on it; it was her hard-earned money. He wasn't very financially supportive of her, don't get me wrong, he was a very good provider and did the best they could given the circumstances, bringing up 5 children, and we didn't go without. She always felt that he was the one giving the pocket money to the grandchildren, although it was from both of them. Now she had some control again. She had her own savings. It was only from her sale at boot sales craft fares, and she kept it for her family. She hardly ever spent it on herself; it was always spent on others.

I remember once, not long after I had moved out of home, and I needed to buy a dressing table. She said to choose one. I asked her why she said, "Just choose one." Back then, they weren't so expensive, in the 80s. "Choose something for about £60," she said, "or if it cost more, I will put £60 towards it." I kept asking her why and she had a smirk on her face. "Just choose something." I thought she must have had a voucher or something, as I didn't want her spending her own money on it, and they had already bought us something for our flat at the time, so I thought she must have a voucher. She pretended it was, so just to get me to buy a dressing table.

Eventually, I found one, and she insisted she come with me. With what I thought was a voucher she had. When it came to it, it was £60 cash. "Here," she said, "I found it in your room in the bin, in one of your payslip envelopes". In those days, we got paid in cash, sometimes with the payslip in a little brown envelope. My mum always tore things up into neat piles, and on this occasion, she found this with the money in it. She didn't think of herself; she thought of me. What I could use it for, and make good use of it, rather than give it to me to waste, as I loved to spend on clothes and shoes then, she made sure I got something good out of it. And I really appreciated it. I would have loved her to have kept it, of course, but she wouldn't.

♥

Going back, organising her surprise 65th party was great, and for once, she had nothing to do with it, as she knew nothing about it. She always looked so glamorous. We let our dad in on the secret but not all of it, as he would blab. He had to be in on the address book and calling her friends. She had lots of friends and was very popular. She never forgot a birthday and loved to write letters, keeping in touch with friends and relatives all over the world. It showed as so many turned up for her birthday from all parts of the UK.

The surprise we kept from my dad was that we arranged for a white Rolls Royce Silver Cloud to pick them up. Someone I knew was a chauffeur and did weddings, and we asked him if he would do it; we paid, of course. He was very professional and came to the front door in his smart uniform and hat, and my dad laughed and loved it too. My mum felt like royalty. She loved every minute of it and seeing her with all her lovely friends turning up; they were like little girls again.

♥

Cooking lessons. "Its time you learned to cook for your husbands." She said, but aiming the demand to me. She insisted on teaching me how to cook as she heard we were quite keen on having takeaways. I could actually cook, but we did love a takeaway. It was easier, especially after a long day at work, and then it was easy to pop out to an Indian restaurant or call for a takeaway. She loved to teach. I wrote everything down as we went through it, getting told off all the time as we did, but I kept my notes and made some fabulous curries. Of course, there was a competition between my mum and dad when it came to cooking a curry. He uses the powder mix; she used fresh.

♥

She loved her grandchildren. Every one of them was special to her in their different ways. She would look around for suitable gifts and really think about what she bought for each of them.

Her first grandchild was a boy, and he loved to do things with acting and theatre. He would put on shows for the family, as did the granddaughters when they came along. She would love to spend hours showing them how to do crafts and cooking and teaching them historical facts about life.

When my son and his younger cousin, my nephew, came along later in life, it was nice to have boys, and they were quite mischievous. Although my mum was quite prudish in her ways, they

138

actually brought her out of herself, and she and my dad really enjoyed their company as they would have sleepovers and loved spending time with their grandparents, who were so much fun. My dad was totally in his element as he could show them how to box and keep fit with weights. Much to my mother's dismay. She would roll her eyes when he would boast about how many trophies he had for boxing when he was young and how handsome he was. My mother would never agree to that, of course. I think my mum admired the straightforwardness of the boys when they spoke. Of course, they respected their grandparents, but they would also ask questions that we would never have asked anyone, let alone our parents or grandparents. But they asked with total innocence and my mum being a very straightforward person, admired this. My dad would make up different stories about how many elephants he fought off in India and how many tigers he fought with one hand tied behind his back. They believed him, as we did growing up too.

It was nice to see how my mum had become so much softer, and it really suited her. My dad had retired, and they would spend hours of fun together with the boys. The boys had their tents in the garden, and my dad had his own tent. He would sneak in at night and leave them in the garden and then make animal noises. He was so young at heart, but my mum was always sensible. I remember once when my son and nephew came into the room. My nephew went over to kiss my mum, and my son pulled down his tracksuit bottoms. My mum and dad laughed so much. My mum would not have been very amused by that in the past; she would have told them off and said how disgusting it was. Boys will be boys. They would spend hours talking, sometimes into the early morning. I think it was a time for my mum to catch up on the gossip, too, as well as teach them lessons of wisdom for life, which they have never forgotten.

Grandparents are great for that. And grandchildren treasure those memories.

As I said before, She never wore anything other than face powder and lipstick. Never used creams, only soap and water. In her latter days, she only used lipstick when someone was coming over or if she was going out. Not even face powder anymore. She loved her pearl earrings and neckless; and a broach.

She eventually stopped colouring her hair in her late 80s, and her grey hair suited her beautiful blue eyes. Her skin was soft, and wrinkles started appearing because she was losing weight. Not because of her age, as she had very good skin and not many wrinkles when she was in her 80s; she said it was all down to not using rubbish on her face.

All her life was order. She had lists of everything and labels. Her jars of spices she kept and just refilled. Old mustard jars. Flora dishes were kept, and if she gave you some food to take home, it was always put in flora cartons which were stacked up in her cupboard, and she was always asked for them back. We felt so guilty if we threw them away. Not that she would have known anyway, but it got to the stage when I had to, as I kept forgetting to take them back, and my kitchen or car boot was filling up with empty flora cartons to return. It was some sort of emotional blackmail. I had to break it in the end. Yes, I am throwing away flora containers and wrapping paper and cellophane from cards. It feels good. It just goes to show that when the family were clearing out the house, it was full of old paper bags and tags and ironed wrapping paper, which was never used. But she did inspire and encourage us in a lot of other ways.

♥

I remember it was coming up to my mum and dad's 70th wedding anniversary, which is really something special to celebrate. As I said before, my mum didn't give any cards to my dad for as far back as I can remember. I said to her, "Mum, I know you haven't given dad a card for years, but as it's going to be your 70th Wedding Anniversary, would you like to give him one? I will get one for you." To my absolute surprise, she said yes, and she continued to say, "But nothing with lots of words in it, just a simple one." In other words, nothing sloshy that says how lovely he is or how in love she is with him. I did get a lovely card for her to give him and also one for him to give her, as they were too old and frail to go out to the shops.

When my mum came to writing it, as it was hard for her to see because of her cataracts that she didn't have done, because she didn't have an opticians appointment for 20 years, she held the pen, and I guided her bony arthritic little finger to the page, and she used her finger as a guide with the pen. As I read it, she wrote, "My dear Mauci". "Mauici" I questioned. "Yes, that is what I used to call him." Ahh, they had nicknames for each other; she must have loved him to do that. We never ever heard or knew about her calling him Mauci. She continued to write, "Thank you for all you did.." I said oh, how lovely, mum" and she continued writing "…n't do for me." "Mum, you can't say that!" but she ignored me and continued with the sentence "and for all you did". Ahh, that's better. How sweet it was and what a privilege, another thing she did, as though she knew

141

that was the last opportunity for her to give him a card, this side of Heaven.

My dad was so pleased with the card he couldn't believe it himself. He always gave her beautiful cards, as I have mentioned, and he would always write a special poem in each card. I was recently looking through some of my mum's autograph books which were signed by her school friends when she left school. I couldn't believe it when I saw that my dad had also signed it, and in the book, he wrote the same poem that he has been writing in her cards ever since:

> "To Glen, The hours I spent with you dear heart,
> are like a string of pearls to me,
> I count them everyone apart, my Rosary, my Rosary.
> With best wishes.
> M.N. James. Dated 30 November 1945"

Also, on the actual day of their 70th Wedding Anniversary, we had arranged for a special card to be sent to them signed by the Queen. They were so proud to have the card; it really meant a lot to them. Although, on the day that it arrived, my mum didn't realise it was even there. She said someone knocked at the door, but she didn't answer it. It was a couple of days later that she opened some of the mail she had, and there was the card from the Queen. Apparently, a postman knocks and says that it is a special delivery from Buckingham Palace. So the moment was lost there, as my mum didn't want to answer the door. But they didn't mind; they loved the card.

So, overall, summing up, I look back now as an adult and see the challenges my mother went through. I haven't mentioned a lot of what she went through in this book, but I know most of them made her the way she used to be before her Miracle. She also felt unloved underneath and had something happen that I haven't mentioned in this book that affected her for most of her life and which would have added to the depression she suffered, which, thankfully, she found peace about after her Miracle. She had to be strong and have a lot of courage to get to where she did. Knowing that she was loved by God, and He gave her a Miracle, and cared about her, meant so much to her that I cannot find words to express it. To see how she changed so much is a miracle in itself.

Chapter 29

Touched by the Holy Spirit

Take note on what is going on around you, or you could miss something very significant, or you may just put it down to something else. That feeling, that gut feeling, our inner consciousness, God has created within us all. Some of us are more perceptive than others. I have always been interested in what is out there, so much more than this earth that we are spinning on.

Be the rock in your family for God. Who will show them the way if you don't. No matter what opposition you come up with from anyone, keep persevering. Don't give up. You will see amazing things, and God will give you the strength and power, and wisdom to fulfil His plans.

We rely on certain members of our families or certain friends to help us when it comes to things and give advice, which is ok, but why not be the one they rely on to lead them to the Lord. To show them the way of life that God wanted us to have. To Pray and to learn to rely on God for everything.

God may give you one person at a time to help or a few. The amazing things you see happening along the way will be so exciting. I used to have prayer meetings at my house with some wonderful friends from different churches. We had amazing times of prayer and fellowship and saw some miraculous things happening. I will touch more on these times in another book.

♥

I was at a church that I used to go to. It was a Pentecostal church, and people spoke in tongues and stood up and prayed out loud. I loved the worship, and the pastor was very good at the word. I hadn't been for a couple of weeks as it was half term, and we had been away. The worship was beautiful, and they started singing a song called "Come, now is the time to worship". It was such a beautiful song, and while singing and worshipping, I spoke to Jesus and said, "Jesus, I am sorry I haven't been in prayer much this week" I was praying, and I said, just like the words of the song, "Jesus come"; immediately my whole body started shaking, and I fell into my seat, I couldn't stop the tears flooding, and I didn't even have time to think about who was looking at me, I was just consumed in whatever was happening. I kept shaking and crying. While all this was happening, I was aware of a burning in the palm of my hand. My right hand and arm were shaking, and I couldn't stop it, but the burning sensation was like fire in the palm of my right hand. I didn't know what was happening. Eventually, I got up to go to the toilet and get myself together, wondering what on earth was happening, but it was good. When I came out of the toilet, one of the women in the church came up to me; this was at the back of the church. She asked me to pray for her. She said she had an appointment at the doctor the next day for a lump that she had and asked if I could pray for her. I remember putting my hand up, and it was still on fire, and as I was praying, the pastor walked by, but he didn't actually say anything. I later asked him about it, and he asked me to speak to his wife. When I did, she said it was something the church had been praying for. I still wanted someone to explain it all to me, as I needed to know. (A few days later, the woman told me that the lump was nothing to worry about). Praise God.

All I know is the most beautiful divine presence stayed with me for about a week. It was so tangible, as though an Angel was standing behind my right shoulder. Nothing worried me; no one could upset me. I had a permanent smile on my face, and I felt like I was on a cloud. I remember one day, a woman pushed in front of me at the checkout in a shop, and I really didn't care; I let her go, still smiling. Even at home, no one could upset me, and it was as though they knew something was going on, but they couldn't put their finger on it. My right hand and arm would still shake, and my palm still felt like it was on fire.

I eventually went to another Church, where I was baptised in the Holy Spirit in the summer at one of their conventions and where we also did an Alpha course. This was the Church that held the tent meetings in the park. It was where I first had an encounter with a pastor who was visiting there, which I told you about at the beginning of the book. I knew the pastor there would understand, as he was very connected to God and full of the power of the Holy Spirit. When I asked him, he knew straight away, he said it was the Holy Spirit. He gave me a book to read called 'Holy Fire' by Michael Brown. In there were all the answers to my questions. Most of the people who were filled with the Holy Spirit were shaking and feeling the fire of God. I knew then that I needed to find another church that understood and where I could use the gift God had given me. After a week, I could feel the beautiful, tangible presence drawing away slowly. I wished I had done more about it at the time, but I just felt so wonderful knowing that the presence of God was there. Maybe it was just for a time to help me.

♥

When you know you are walking with God, you will walk with confidence and boldness. You won't have to ask anyone anymore, especially if they don't help. God wants us to look to Him. "Draw nigh to God, and He will draw nigh to you" (James 4:8 KJV) God wants a relationship with us. Direct contact. Or maybe speak to people who you connect to. You will know who they are just by being in the same room; you will be drawn or connected to a child of God who is full of the Holy Spirit.

You can have experiences every day, and as Christians, we should be. If a doctor saw someone with an injury, they would hopefully straight away go to assist, or if someone had first aid experience, they would. As Christians, we are assigned to help others, to show them and be there for them in their time of need and to show them the way of the Lord Jesus Christ.

Discernment. When you go somewhere and don't get a good feeling about it, you should Leave. Or sometimes, you can be in a situation or near someone, and you get a strong uneasy feeling like you really shouldn't be there. God is warning us to be aware. And He protects us. He will.

♥

When I still lived at home, my mum used to be up all hours until I came home. Although I believed totally, I didn't really know about praying for the right man, a Christian; I just lived each day, for each day. If I didn't like a job, I would get a new one. I went through a stage of being very unsettled and found some relationships quite challenging, but through all this, I have gained a lot of experience when it comes to people and life in general. Perhaps that is why God allowed it, so I would be able to help others in all sorts of situations.

Sometimes I think people think I am telling fibs when I say and can relate to things. Oh, she's done everything. It's not that; it is that God has given us the insight to help others. Within the mission, He has for us. Everyone has something unique to them that they are good at. We can't do it all.

Chapter 30

Faith in Action

I have always believed in the healing power of Jesus Christ. The Bible says so, and I believe what the Bible says. I grew up in Sunday school watching the pictures of Jesus healing the sick. He loved everyone. What a lovely man.

I remember one night, feeling a cyst. I began to panic, thinking the worst. Then I thought, No, We have been given the power in the name of Jesus. This was when I learned how to pray in authority. We don't have to beg God; it is already done when Jesus went to the cross for us. He took our infirmities, and by His stripes, we are healed. I held the middle finger on my right hand on the cyst. I prayed, "By the finger of God I cast you out and the kingdom of God has come" (The verse in the Bible says, "But if I cast out demons with the finger of God, surely the kingdom of God has come to you" Luke 11:20 NKJV). I kept praying it over and over again, getting stronger and more determined each time. Eventually, I felt the cyst go down under my finger and flatten to nothing. I got up and praised God. It was the middle of the night, so I was quiet so as not to wake anyone up. I didn't go to the GP the next day, it had gone, but I was curious to find out what it could have been. By going to the GP, I was doubting God I felt; He healed me instantly; why would I want to go and find out what it could have been, they couldn't have told me anything because there was nothing to look at. Praise God. It never came back, whatever it was.

♥

I remember years ago, in my youth in the 70s, we broke down in the middle of the countryside. It was very late at night, and the battery on the pickup truck we were in was totally flat. We tried to jump-start it with a friend's car, but it wouldn't start. We tried for quite a while, but nothing would start it. Jesus was my best friend, and I totally relied on Him for everything. So it was only natural to ask Him to help, and I prayed, "Jesus, please start the engine" it was like a bolt of lightning that hit the bonnet, and when I turned the key, it started like a new engine. The three people with me at the time, were shocked but not surprised because they had seen the answer to prayer many times. They just shook their heads and said, unbelievable. They knew it was God. I am no one special at all; I just totally put my faith and trust in Jesus. He wants to have a relationship with everyone. Only we have to show people the way sometimes.

Chapter 31

Lazarus

My son has a very strong faith. He has also seen many miracles. I remember when he was very young, about 5, he had a goldfish, his first pet. We have always prayed since he was very small. It is so important to teach our children the Word of God and His Power in our lives to help us.

Well, one day, the fish had been floating for a while, not doing much, and it was quite obvious what was going on, so we put it in the garage, which was at the bottom of the garden, in its tank. My son would come home from school and look at his fish. He was a little concerned that it was floating around but somehow thought it would be ok.

After three days, the fish now completely upside down, we knew it was well and truly gone, and it was time to put it to rest.

We had to tell my son when he came in from school about his fish that it had died. Well, he had none of it; he was so upset and wouldn't believe it he ran down the garden to the garage and spent some time in there with his fish.

He later came back about 15 mins later and said, "The fish is going to be all right; I prayed for the fish". Although I believe 100 per cent, I also realise that everything has its time, and perhaps it was time for the fish. We carried on with our evening and didn't look at the fish again.

The next morning, my son went down to the garage, and I followed him. To my surprise, the fish was swimming around like a fresh, healthy fish. We thanked God, although my son didn't expect anything other than to see that. Do you know the fish lived for 13 years. It ended up living in our garden pond with lots of other fish. We should have called it Lazarus.

♥

Another time, we were away in Devon we rented a cottage for the week. We had such a wonderful time with other members of our family as well, and my son and my nephew enjoyed it so much. They were about 7 and 9 at the time. My son asked if we could stay another day. I said no, we had to go. He pleaded and pleaded. I explained about the changeover day, Saturday being the changeover day, and other people would be coming in, so we couldn't stay. He then said to me, "You told me if I pray in faith, it will happen, so I am praying that we can stay another night, and so we will". Mmmmm, ok, God, I looked up; what are we going to do in this situation? I will leave it to you, as always. Well, there happened to be a problem with the washing machine at the cottage, and the people who owned it came to the cottage before we left. My brother-in-law was a plumber, and he offered to fix it, which he did. They were so pleased, the owners, that they said, "if you would like to stay another night, we don't have anyone booked in for next week, so you can stay another night for free for helping to fix the washing machine". God has an amazing way; He never fails, and He answers our prayers. My son prayed in faith, and God never let him down.

Chapter 32

Some have entertained Angels

So, if God's plan was to give my mum her Miracle at that time anyway, it would have happened in the ambulance, and she would have come around as she did, and all would be ok. But what would we have missed in all this. I believe God would have healed her anyway, and if I hadn't been there to witness the presence of God, it could be said that it was just one of those things like the doctor seemed to think, it fixed itself whatever it was, but couldn't have been that serious, which is what he thought. But he didn't see what we saw at the house. And no one would have been any of the wiser. But I knew something was happening in the ambulance. Whether I was there or not, I believe my mum would have been healed because it wasn't her time, and God had this plan for her life already.

My mum said if I wasn't in the ambulance, no one would have known, she would have just thought it was another paramedic, and she wouldn't even have questioned it. But I wouldn't let it go; I kept telling everyone, "something happened in the ambulance; mum was healed in the ambulance" because I felt the Tangible presence of God over her and then saw her change in an instant. Also, the paramedic in the back with me. He would have thought the same as the doctor. He was amazed as it was that she started talking and was sitting up when she got to A&E. He may not have sensed the presence of God; he didn't see the Angel, all he saw was the miraculous change in my mum, which was enough to make him shake his head in amazement and unbelief.

How many times you hear people saying they were so lucky to get out of that one. They were there on their own, but they didn't see the Angel that assisted them. They say it's miraculous, and of course, it was.

I love the testimonies of Angel encounters when people have been under threat, and then the people who have threatened them suddenly run away. When questioned why they ran, they say they saw those huge men standing by them. They were Angels. God is always looking out for us. The people under threat didn't see their huge Angels, but the others did. How many times does this happen in our daily lives, and we just take it for granted, unaware of what is going on around us in the spiritual realm. There are so many amazing Angel encounters happening every second in the world around us.

It has certainly made me realise that when the Bible says He will give his Angels charge over us to protect us wherever we go, He does.

Prayer is powerful. When Jesus prayed for the sick, He had total compassion on them; even though He saw their sins, He didn't want them to suffer. He just said, "Be healed" or "Get up and walk".

Having a personal relationship with Jesus is the best thing in the world. My mum found that out too. It was such a pleasure to see how she really trusted God and also how God loved her and how special she was to Him. Even though she hadn't been to Church every week, she hadn't read her Bible every night. She knew God was in her heart, and He saw her heart.

I don't know how people get through life without having a relationship with God. I saw my mum, a very angry, quite bitter person. She was even angry with God, she said, at times. But after really getting to know Him, not that you need to have a miracle to believe every time, but just having that change in her life, the difference in herself was unbelievable. She didn't get angry so much; she didn't seem to care what was said and didn't bite. In fact, my dad realised it so much I think he would just test her by trying to wind her up. She laughed a lot more and was more loving and caring, and companionate. It was lovely that she actually came to church with us.

Yes, I believe in Angels; you see photos of them all around, in churches, paintings, books everyday life. I know they are there in the Bible, but I never pray to them. My prayer and relationship has always been with Jesus. The Bible says they are here to help us, and the only way is through Jesus. They are spiritual beings sent to help God's children. We are not to worship Angels, and God's Angels will be the first to tell you that, but I am so pleased we have them around us to protect us, sent from God. I sometimes look out of the window and think of the mighty Angels standing around on guard for us. Praise God. What an amazing thought.

So remember the scripture, "Don't forget to entertain strangers, for by so doing some have unwittingly entertained Angels" (Hebrews 13:2 NKJV).

Amen.

Thank you for taking the time to read this book. I hope you have enjoyed it, and that it has been an inspiration to you.

God bless you and your families.

With love

Glenna

"Even to your old age and grey hairs I am He, I am He who will sustain you. I have made you and I will carry you; I will sustain you and I will rescue you". (Isaiah 46:4 NIV)

Glenna, celebrating her 90th Birthday.

www.ingramcontent.com/pod-product-compliance
Lightning Source LLC
Chambersburg PA
CBHW061517050726
47593CB00002B/620